ANTON CHEKHOV

ANTON CHEKHOV

THE VOICE OF TWILIGHT RUSSIA

By

Princess Nina Andronikova Toumanova

*Kinder, macht Neues, Neues und abermal
Neues! Hängt ihr euch ans Alte, so hat
euch der Teufel der Inproductivität, und
ihr seit die traurigsten Künstler*

—RICHARD WAGNER

COLUMBIA UNIVERSITY PRESS
New York · Morningside Heights

CC

LC37010194

Foreword

IT GIVES me great pleasure to introduce to the reader this excellent book on Chekhov by Princess Nina Andronikova Toumanova, which presents a very interesting study of one of the most original Russian writers.

The charming figure of Chekhov is sharply outlined against the historical background, shown in the true perspective. The author displays a keen observation in depicting "that yesterday which seems to be separated from our own day by centuries." We follow with interest the transition of the gay young Chekhov with his buffoonery to the Chekhov of the later years, complex and profound, combining in his writing the motifs of *Holy Russia* with philosophical thoughts and with the everyday occurrences of his own epoch.

The chapters on the theatre are particularly interesting, for the author believes that this form of art presents "one of the most brilliant and important pages of Russian culture." She points out that Chekhov's plays summarize several decades of Russian history, which she describes as a period of a long twilight.

The book is charming and intelligent. The most pronounced gifts of the author are her clear thinking and her ability to express her thoughts in precise and well-chosen words. She is a born linguist and writer. Her knowledge of the language, literature, and history of several European countries is remarkable, as also is her sense of color and style. Long travels and serious study have given her an interesting personality that combines modern efficiency with the profound culture that is acquired only in families through the course of centuries. The family of the Princes Andronikov is very old and descends, according to the tradition, from Andronikos Komnenos, Emperor of Byzantium (1183-1185). His son Alexios, after the massacre of his family in Constantinople, established himself in Georgia (the Colchis of the ancients), a mighty kingdom at that time united to Byzantium by the Christian faith and also, probably, by family ties of the rulers. The descendants of Alexios assumed the name of Andronikos as their family name. Princess Andronikova Toumanova was born in Georgia but spent the greater part of her life in France, where she began her academic career in the Law School at the University of Paris. Several years ago she came to America, unable to speak English at all, and succeeded, despite the most adverse circumstances, in presenting an excellent dissertation, written in her spare hours, mostly at night. We can only admire the iron will and the never-broken spirit which she inherited from her ancestors and hope that this, her first book in English, will be followed by others of equal value.

A. VASILIEV

THE UNIVERSITY OF WISCONSIN
    November, 1936

Preface

CHEKHOV, the creator of a new form of art, may be regarded as a precursor of a long row of brilliant writers who flourished between 1895 and 1915 in Russia. To the casual reader Chekhov's literary activity appears to be separated into two distinct phases; the writing of the last decade seems to have little in common with the short humorous tales of the early '80s. The student of Chekhov, however, may easily discern from the very beginning a creative talent of the highest order, permeated with deep sympathy for humanity, and may trace simultaneously the nascence of the mood which represents a unique page in the history of Russian letters. The works of Anton Chekhov cannot be understood without the knowledge of his life and illness reflected in his stories and plays. Therefore, the aim of this volume is to give his biography parallel with the development of the mood, the elusive charm of which has never been surpassed or even imitated.

My chief sources of information, besides the intense study of Chekhov's literary works, were his numerous letters, the memoirs of his brothers and his friends, the biography by Izmailov, and many articles which were available to me in the New York Public Library, in the Library of Columbia University, in the Russian (Turgenev) Library in Paris, and in the Public Library of Los Angeles.

In my endeavor to understand Chekhov the man, I have

been very fortunate in my travels — from New York to San Francisco, in Paris, London, Geneva, and Rome — in running across my compatriots, scattered all over the globe, who told me some charming bits about Chekhov, gathered from his relatives and his friends. In Algiers I met once an old Russian physician who was bound for Egypt as I was. He had personally known Chekhov and admired him deeply as a writer and a man. As we sat on the hot sand of the Lybian desert, gazing on the inscrutable, mysterious face of the Sphynx, we were discussing the author of *The Cherry Garden*, who in the shadow of imminent death had never given up his quest after some deeper meaning of life.

To all those friends of an hour, whose names I have forgotten and who verbally rendered me great assistance, I owe profound thanks.

I am deeply indebted to the late Count Ilya Tolstoy, who told me how his great father appreciated Chekhov, the perfect story-teller, particularly his stories "The Darling" and "In Court"; to Constantine Stanislavsky, who made me understand Chekhov the playwright; to Prince Zurab Avalov, who gave me many invaluable hints; to Professor Jules Legras in Paris, who had twice visited Chekhov at his estate near Moscow and described to me their meetings; and to Prince Sviatopolk-Mirsky, who encouraged me in my pursuit. From all those long talks, more than out of books, emerged clearly the living and pulsating personality of this great Russian writer, who became to me a dear old friend known for many years.

I am anxious to express my sincere gratitude to Professors Alexander Vasiliev, Arthur Livingston, Clarence Manning, and John Dyneley Prince, whose unalterable kindness kept up my spirits in dark moments of fatigue and distress.

Preface

In giving the quotations from Chekhov's plays, I used the translations of Marian Fell and Julius West with some modification. All the other quotations I have translated myself, unless otherwise indicated in the footnotes. My chief difficulty lay in the spelling of Russian titles and words in Latin characters. I am fully aware that "Mysliashchie Realisty," "V Sumerkakh," "Nevinnia Riechi" may perplex the American reader, not only because they interrupt the narrative, but also because they have the frightening aspect of some prehistoric animal, a sort of a shapeless ichthyosaur, unpleasant to the eye, whereas in Russian the same words look peaceful, domestic, and soothing. Also the writing of proper names often tends to confusion, for there are no definite rules for transliteration.

Here and there I have given a brief exposition of Russian history which may help the Western reader to understand better the epoch in which Chekhov lived and wrote.

N. A. T.

Columbia University
November, 1936

Contents

Illustrations

ANTON CHEKHOV

I

Introduction

IN THE spring of 1894, Chekhov wrote to his faithful
old friend Suvorin: "I began to believe in progress in my
early childhood, because of the tremendous difference
between the time when I was still whipped and the time
when I was not." Progress was, indeed, a word to conjure
with in the '60s and '70s, when young Chekhov first con-
sciously viewed this ever-changing world. Although a true
son of his epoch, utterly permeated with scientific materialism, Anton Pavlovich had just as little in common
with the utilitarian, aggressive '60s as he had with the
populist movement of the philanthropic and sentimental
'70s.

Overanxious about the architectural perfection and the
musically fluid construction of his stories, highly gifted
and original, Chekhov refused to tread the beaten path.
He was one of the first to believe in artistic economy and
to represent an aesthetic revival in that period, when
realism supplied the leading motive in all forms of art.
Small wonder, then, that the venerable writer, Grigorovich, on reading the delightful short tales, "no longer
than a sparrow's nose,"[1] that flooded the humorous maga-

---

[1] Chekhov's own words in Kuprin's recollections in *Chekhovskii sbornik*
(Chekhov Miscellany) , p. 123.

zines of the early '8os, promptly recognized a rising new star in the literary skies of Russia.

The greater speed of life towards the end of the nineteenth century was inevitably reflected in literature in the form of short stories; their laconic precision was quite in tune with the times. In France, the short story appears to have had an inherent correspondence with the national genius from the days of the fabliaux. In Russian literature, however, this type is primarily associated with the name of Chekhov. In this particular field he overshadowed even the greatest of his predecessors.[2] It is possible that he was encouraged in his pursuit of a succinct literary form by the aesthetic realism of Maupassant, whose works were highly appreciated in Russia.[3] Yet there is a great difference between the French and the Russian masters. Love intrigue, often to the detriment of good taste, is the invariable theme with the more colorful Maupassant, who scorns life for its meaninglessness. Avoiding crudity of color and speech, Chekhov, always charitable, never expresses indignation but responds to hope, to sorrow, and to happiness and represents the human soul in all its multiform aspects.

Leo Tolstoy, who greatly admired both of them, said: "Chekhov, I think, is an incomparable artist. If he resembles anyone it is Maupassant. As an artist Chekhov could never be compared with previous Russian writers, such as Turgenev, Dostoyevsky, or myself. He has his own form as an impressionist."[4]

[2] There are short stories by Pushkin — *Tales of Belkin* — and by Lermontov — "Taman'" (this Chekhov considered a masterpiece). Gogol wrote "The Portrait" and his famous "The Cloak" and is to be counted a direct ancestor not only of Chekhov but also of Dostoyevsky. See, finally, Turgenev, *A Sportsman's Sketches*.

[3] Said Chekhov, "It is hard for one to work, Maupassant's mastery has set such high standards for us. Yet it is necessary, especially for us Russians, and we must be courageous in our work." Bunin, V, 297.

[4] Sergeyenko's recollections, in *Niva*, July, 1904, pp. 250-52. Gerhardi,

Thus Chekhov appears as the creator of a new genre in Russia — the short story, in which he outlines his subject with quick, masterful strokes, emphasizing only a few distinctive traits. This translation of reality into artistic images that possess definite and precise contours is impressive. It has somewhat the effect of a delicate etching.

An amusing anecdote, often an actual happening, is the basis of Chekhov's short story. He relates it impersonally, with aloofness and apparent indifference, the impassive attitude of a physician. Chekhov always keeps the sense of objective evaluation in his tales, even when he is describing himself or putting his own thoughts in the mouths of his heroes. He always considered reality as though he were looking down on it from a mountain top, and he drew the different patterns of life in definite perspective, viewing them, as it were, through a powerful lens.

His intimate knowledge of every side of life allowed him to bring many new features into literature, and his numerous tales touch upon all phases of the tragic human drama. His characters are not invented; they are taken from his environment. In his gallery of portraits, one finds monks, peasants, teachers, doctors, landowners — all types he knew to perfection. Usually they are unimportant, unhappy people, often very intelligent but deprived of will. They do things they dislike and, never living fully, regret only the swift passage of their lives.

The pictures Chekhov drew are depressing and gloomy; he never pretended to teach how to live. He was a great master of the pen with the gift for transforming even trivial things into works of art. He had the observant analytical mind of the physician, which enabled him to

pp. 96-97, disagrees with Tolstoy: "The comparison with Maupassant is a little naïve. One could understand Maupassant being called the French Chehov, in a mood of generous extravagance. But it was well meant; and after all Maupassant preceded Chehov, and both of them excelled in the short story . . ."

penetrate the inner realms of human hearts and understand the secret motives of human emotions. On first realizing the futility of existence, Chekhov experienced a profound sorrow. Later in his career, though still perplexed by the mystery of fleeting life, he became resigned to the inevitable and passed from the black fits of despair that beset his youth to the serenity of his last days.

Though he learned to trace emotional processes with medical precision and so came to acquire a deep understanding of the *genus homo,* Chekhov never attained the towering greatness of Tolstoy or of Dostoyevsky. He lacked the heroism present in those others, a heroism that consisted in fighting Philistinism and exposing it with merciless clarity, in rebelling against the pettiness of everyday life, in endeavoring to surmount difficulties. Chekhov is a great artist using a small canvas, a poet of the little. His characters invariably submit, on the plea that the weak are always morally superior to the efficient. There are no real heroes in his works. The central figures all stand on a par, all conveying a painful feeling of misunderstanding and sorrow.

In this Chekhov proved himself a true son of his generation. The '80s and '90s mark the degeneration of the hero. They lack men of action. They represent a slowing down of the literary pulse and the general lassitude of the *fin de siècle,* which was followed by dissatisfaction and gloom. This lack of ideals, of romantic dreams, led to a state of passive despair, tinged with a dim hope that perhaps "in two or three hundred years life on earth will become unspeakably beautiful."[5]

Chekhov's plays occupy a special place in the history of the theatre. Believing that life should be so interpreted

[5] Chekhov's own words. Colonel Vershinin, a character in *The Three Sisters* uses the same expression.

that the audience would divine the inner and greater realities born in the mind of the author, Chekhov expressed the subtle aspects of human nature: its complete aloneness, the disintegration that overtakes a human soul immersed in its own agony. His unheroic heroes, who live in a strange world of keyed-up emotions, are, like himself, perpetually puzzled by life. The dramatic dialogue disappears, to give place to a peculiar form of speech built along two parallel lines that never meet. One is constantly aware of an undertone of sorrow and pain expressed in detached, inconsistent, often incoherent words. Long pauses and reticence create an odd feeling that important things, indeed the most important ones, have never been said and never will be said. The actions of his heroes are as surprisingly inadequate as their conversation. Often in the midst of a desperate situation they smile and cling to hope, for hope is the only resource of those charming misfits. They are never able to fight.

The form of Chekhov's plays is essentially static. He has interwoven symbols into their outwardly realistic structure, not only as a rebellion against the artificiality and the platitudes of his time, but as the means of creating a misty autumnal mood, his favorite artistic effect. Moonbeams on the lake, fallen leaves, abandoned gardens, empty houses, an odd stillness interrupted only by "a sound sad and strange, as if coming from the sky" form an appropriate autumnal setting for his forlorn heroes, with their tears, their longing for the unattainable, and their final partings which are as tragic as death.

This strange mixture of symbolism and reality, of hope and despair, born of the realization of his own ever-growing illness and intensified by a political and literary stagnation that lasted for decades, created that peculiar "Chekhovian mood" which began a new page in the literary history of crepuscular Russia. Maxim Gorky defined it thus: "Reading Anton Tchekhov's stories, one feels oneself in a melancholy day of late autumn. . . . Everything is strange, lonely, motionless, helpless."[6]

Indeed, it was in a queer world of silvery twilight and dark shadows that the gentle soul of Chekhov took refuge, in a desperate fear of life.

[6] Gorky, "Anton Tchekhov: Fragments of Recollections," p. 106.

BOOK I

The Days of Antosha Chekhonte

II

Awakening

THE city of Taganrog, later so proud of Anton Chekhov, was quite unperturbed on January 17, 1860, when a little boy was born in the family of a grocer. The father of this boy, Pavel Iegorovich Chekhov, was a typical man of the working class, brought up as a serf, deprived of education, yet gifted and very religious. Taking his duties as a *pater familias* seriously, he ruled his household with an iron hand and inspired in his children nothing but fear.

Anton's mother, Evgenia Yakovlevna Morosova, was one of those rare women who invariably radiate happiness and warmth. She had received some education in the household of her father, a cloth merchant. Spiritually superior to her environment, she found ways to hold the family together, to give her children a pleasant home despite the tyranny of her husband, and to instill in their young souls the mutual affection, gentleness, and kindness characteristic of all the Chekhovs. She appreciated the beauty of the world, loved flowers and animals, and was compassionate towards the defenseless and unhappy — traits which she transmitted to her son Anton, along with her charming disposition. An excellent storyteller, she would relate in picturesque terms the varied episodes of her husband's and her own life: their long journey from her distant native town to Taganrog across the immense plains of Russia, the hardships of serfdom, the Crimean War.

Her only rival in storytelling was the children's nurse, Agatha Kumskaya, who like Pushkin's Arina Rodionovna[1] and many another old nurse of those bygone days, lived in the peculiar world of Russian folklore and folk poetry, peopled by witches, monsters, and ravished princesses. Both mother and nurse loved to tell stories.[2] A reminiscent epic of the bombardment of Taganrog would be followed by the fairy tale of the beautiful Maria Marevna, who was seized by the skeleton-like monster, Koshchey, and was saved by Ivan the Tsarevich, the Russian Parsifal, simpleton and hero. The children listened for hours to the rhythmic flow of these stories and so experienced a fascination known to all Russians from the prince in his palace to the mujik in his lowly hut.

Harsh though he was, Anton's father nevertheless showed artistic tendencies. He had learned to paint and to play the violin, and, like his compatriots, he passionately loved music, especially church chorals; his day began and ended with song. As leader of the choir, he always went with his family to early Mass and his sons sang under his direction. They used to go to the chapel of the palace where Emperor Alexander I had died mysteriously in 1825.

Returning home, they would practice new hymns. It was a zealous but untrained choir. Pavel Iegorovich

[1] Pushkin's famous nurse who shared with him his forced seclusion in Mikhailovskoe in 1825 and cheered his wearisome hours by telling him fairy tales that were eventually to become masterpieces under the pen of that greatest of Russian poets.

[2] The story "Schast'e" (Happiness, 1889) was told to Chekhov by his nurse, Agatha. Chekhov dedicated it to the poet Polonsky (1819-1898), considering it as his best: "The steppe, the night, and then the pale dawn in the east, a flock of sheep and three human figures discussing happiness." So he wrote to Polonsky, March 25, 1888.

Chekhov, however, was endowed with an exceptional musical ear, led as well as he could, and cuffed his children whenever they sang off key. In the evening the family gathered for the reading of the *Chetyi Minei*, a popular book on the lives of the saints found in patriarchal households of those days.[3] Here in succession appeared St. Nicholas, St. George, and the other beloved saints deeply rooted in Russian religious thought. Before retiring, the Chekhovs said long prayers to the Savior and to the Blessed Virgin. The next day started again with an early Mass.

This enforced religious education, at the expense of freedom and play, was most distasteful to the boys. Anton would often say to his brothers: "What an unhappy lot we are! Other boys may run, play, visit their friends. We can only go to church."[4] And unwillingly he went to church, unwillingly he kissed the hand of the priest, and when he sang he felt like a "little convict."[5] Kneeling before the altar, exposed to the eyes of strangers in his shabby clothes and his worn shoes, the boy suffered tortures of humiliation. His diffidence was undoubtedly born of those agonizing moments, together with the almost pathological self-consciousness that later became so characteristic of his heroes.

To the end of his days Chekhov remembered the church ritual perfectly and, as the years went by and the painful memories of his boyhood faded, he came to be deeply touched by the beauty of the Greco-Russian rite, by the exquisite singing, and by the profound poetry of its

[3] *Menologia*, in Russian *Chetyi Minei*. It is a book of saints' lives composed by Macarius, Metropolitan of Moscow, in the sixteenth century and revised by Demetrius of Rostov a century later.

[4] Alexander Chekhov, "Chekhov pievchii" (Chekhov the Singer), in *Viestnik Evropy* (Messenger of Europe), Oct., 1907.

[5] Chekhov to his friend Ivan Shcheglov, March 9, 1892.

prayers. In his mature years he loved to go to vespers, and "create themes for sweet songs in the semi-darkness of the galleries and arches."

Above all he loved church bells. He would go to the Stone Bridge in Moscow or would listen to them from his study window with delight. In a letter to Suvorin (December 5, 1895) he said: "I got up early, lighted the candles, and started to write while the chimes were ringing — it was pleasant." Yet most of the thrashings he received in his early childhood were for poor singing or for misconduct during religious ceremonies. He never became a devout man.

Unpleasant as were these associations, they were not the only hardships of the young Chekhovs, as we learn from the autobiographical story, "Three Years": "My father began to teach me, or more exactly to whip me, when I was not even five. . . . Every morning, upon awakening, I used to ask myself whether or not I should be whipped that day. . . . I was taken to the store when I was hardly eight years old and worked there like an ordinary grocer's boy."[6]

The strict Pavel Iegorovich lived according to the *Domostroy*.[7] He thought it necessary to make children work, not realizing the harm that he was doing to their young souls. He would interrupt their play to send them to the grocery store to "learn the trade," and Antosha, "with tears in his eyes," would shiver for hours on duty, selling carrots and sugar, in company with two frightened little boys, apprentices to his exacting father.[8] Their evil

[6] "Tri Goda" (Three Years), Marks edition of the complete works of Chekhov, X, 104-5.

[7] *Domostroy* (The Home Orderer) a book written by the monk Sylvester in 1566. It gave general rules for the guidance of heads of families.

[8] Alexander Chekhov, "Anton Tchekhov — Shopkeeper," in Koteliansky, tr. and ed., *Anton Tchekhov, Literary and Theatrical Reminiscences*, p. xxii.

fate he commemorated in two sad but delightful stories, "Van'ka" (1886), and "Sleepy" (1888), and his own unhappy memories prompted him to say many years later, "I never knew a real childhood."[9] Yet in that hateful store, which he remembered all his life with horror, Chekhov developed his amazing keenness of observation.

It was a sort of local club. Every day the multicolored, talkative, typically southern population of that lazy provincial town passed before his eyes: street jesters showing their tricks and telling amusing and not always polite stories, traveling monks begging for alms "for the Holy Mount Athos," pilgrims bound for the Holy Land—a swarm of wanderers, characteristic of restless Russia. There he heard the gossip, the quarrels, and the popular jokes with their incisive vocabulary. All these things gave the gifted boy indelible memories that were finally to take concrete form in many of his tales.[10]

In the '60s Taganrog was inhabited almost exclusively by Greeks. They monopolized all the business and were rich and influential. Pavel Iegorovich considered them good people to cultivate, and expected his sons to become clerks in some of the innumerable Greek concerns. The boys, therefore, were forced to master the language and, from the beginning, to make contact with Greeks.

There was a parish school in Taganrog called impressively "The School of the Emperor Constantine." The headmaster was a Greek, Nicholas Vutsinas, who had left sunny shores haunted by the shades of Pythagoras and Plato to try his luck in the barbaric land of the Scyths,

[9] Chekhov to his brother Alexander, April 4, 1892.
[10] A strong imprint of Taganrog is to be noted in "Step'" (The Steppe, 1888); "Ogni" (The Lights, 1888); "Stary Dom" (The Old House, 1889); "Zhena" (The Wife, 1892); "Palata No. 6" (Ward No. 6, 1892); and "Ionych" (1898); The Greek Dymba, hero of "Svad'ba" (The Wedding, 1889), actually lived in Taganrog.

where he arrived "without trousers," to use an expression of his own. That worthy son of Homer was entrusted with the task of spreading the light of learning among the children of his compatriots for the sum of twenty-five rubles per annum. His school was a large, untidy room with rows of desks. Vutsinas had pupils of all kinds, though they came not so much to learn as to free their parents from the burden of supervision. Ragged, shaggy, disheveled, they looked like so many little bandits and paid a noisy and mocking welcome to their new comrades, "Nicolaos and Antonios Tsekoff," who were to bear the ordeal of two long years among them.

Vutsinas brought with him the customs of pastoral Hellas. After a few admonitions, oral and manual, he would withdraw to a neighboring room and go peacefully to sleep, leaving his charges to enter the lofty spheres of knowledge by their own devices. Warfare would soon break out among these Greek heroes, but it never succeeded in awaking the philosophical schoolmaster. When his snoring became unmistakably sonorous, they forgot for a while "the wrath of Achilles against Agamemnon, King of Men," made common cause, left the classroom by the window, took the neighboring orchard by assault, overthrew the sentry-box, rang the bell in the house of the police officer, and then ran for safety through the silent streets of sleepy Tanganrog.

The school made a terrible impression on the sensitive little Chekhov. All his life, despite a kindly understanding nature, he cherished an unspeakable aversion for everything Greek. In one of his beautiful stories, "Uchitel' Slovesnosti" (The Teacher of Literature, 1889), he mentioned as an embodiment of pedagogical stupidity "a teacher of Greek," who was a weakling, "devoid alike of intellect and personality." Shortly before his death, on learning that several of his tales had been translated into Greek, he confessed that he had forgotten every word of that language.

This "legendary education" might have lasted much longer and would probably have culminated in some minor clerkship in a Greek firm had it not been for the insistence of his intelligent, far-seeing mother, Evgenia Yakovlevna Chekhova, who finally persuaded her stubborn husband that knowledge was important in equipment for life. Two years later (1868) the boys were transferred to the Classical Gymnasium in Taganrog, a tremendous step forward, since the secondary as well the higher education in Russia was very good.

Little Anton continued, meantime, to work in the grocery store, studying his lessons behind the counter. Fearing that he might remain a grocer forever, the boy who was to become one of the ten best writers in Russia[11] decided to learn some other trade. He chose tailoring and eventually supplied his favorite brother Nikolay with a pair of trousers so tight that Nikolay was nicknamed "Macaroni" by the naughty boys on the streets. This venture into manual labor was, however, the first and the last in the life of Chekhov.

Anton was then a "nice easy-going fellow" with the smiling disposition of his mother. In his spare hours he would run down to the sea and play games, more to please his friends than himself. While his sturdy little body grew healthy and strong in the invigorating air of that quiet southern town, he was neither very noisy nor very lively, in his quietness exemplifying the proverbial Little Russian type, for Little Russians are nationally known for their laziness.

He liked best to tell stories. These were so funny as to

[11] Mirsky, *Contemporary Russian Literature*, p. 96.

keep his whole class laughing, while he would maintain perfect impassivity himself. Endowed with keen observation, he would summarize a situation or bring out a salient trait in a single witty word. He had a notebook in which he set down no end of amusing tales, found no one knew where. Eventually the pupils' noisy gaiety would attract the attention of a teacher, the book would be confiscated, and soon in the teacher's room the gray-haired disciplinarians would be laughing as heartily as the rogues under their charge.

Antosha's other great gift was improvisation, which gave rise to many of his tales. Inexhaustible in invention, he was an accomplished mimic, and there were not a few "funny numbers" in his wide repertoire. One of his subjects was the military governor of the province as he appeared in gala uniform in the cathedral on official holidays. Girded with an old cavalry sabre Antosha delivered a little speech with all the solemn mannerism of that general. Sometimes when he imitated an aged deacon of the town church, his chubby young face would seem to become worn and old, he would stretch his neck to grotesque thinness and, in a sniffling voice, recite some bit from the service.

His masterpiece, however, represented a scene in a dentist's office. His brother Alexander would appear with a bandaged cheek, screaming at the top of his voice. Looking very much the respectable dentist, Antosha would meticulously arrange his "instruments" and then, after many mishaps, amid ear-rending screams from the patient, take a pair of tongs and extract the tooth — a huge cork — from his brother's mouth, finally presenting it to his audience as the latest "triumph of surgery."

"Khirurgia" (Surgery), in fact, became the theme and the title of an amusing early tale of Chekhov and in this

his "dentist's act" remained unchanged. So in "Kanitel'"
(Dawdle) he used a modified version of his deacon, a
fussy old sacristan who quite loses his way among the
details of his daily routine. Though very short, these
stories are full of sparkling wit and youthful exuberance.
They cannot be disregarded in spite of their buffoonery,
for they are authentic "slices of life" transformed into
artistic imagery. Unfortunately, they lose much in translation, so colloquial and so typically Russian are their
jokes.

At the Gymnasium Antosha kept his watchful eyes open,
noticing many odd traits imperceptible to others. Naturally he accepted the age-old school tradition that has
survived from the ancient palaestra down to our times —
he made fun of his teachers. Later he utilized these early
impressions in beautiful tales, "The Teacher of Literature" and also in "The Man in the Case,"[12] with its com-
posite portrait having particular reference to the inspector,
A. F. Diakonov, a dried-up creature with nothing human
about him, who wore galoshes, carried an umbrella on
the brightest summer days, and always had cotton in his
ears.

Though a mediocre student much more interested in
life than in books, Antosha was liked by all his teachers.
He had the radiant charm that even in his "autumnal
days" was to attract many warm friends. What is surprising is that, despite their affection for him through all his
eleven years in the Gymnasium, his teachers never discovered in him anything exceptional.[13] Father Pokrovsky,
who taught religion, was perhaps the only one to sense
something out of the ordinary in the attractive youth. That

[12] "Chelovek v Futliare" (1898).
[13] It is interesting to note that Balzac was also considered a mediocrity by
his teachers.

gay and lively priest was pleased with the boy's knowledge of the ritual and of many Slavonic texts and appreciated his wit and gaiety. He had a way of calling him "Chekhonte" in jest, pronouncing the word with a singing intonation natural to a priest accustomed to chanting the services. This affectionate alteration of the name of Chekhov has no particular meaning. Such was the origin of a pseudonym which was to become dear to all Russia, associated with the joyful laughter that marks the first period of Chekhov's literary career. "Chekhonte" liked the kind priest and years after he left Taganrog occasionally inquired after him in his usual jesting manner: "How is Father Pokrovsky? Has he not yet joined a regiment of hussars?"[14]

It may have been due to Father Pokrovsky that Chekhov always retained a liking for odd names, peculiar in sound or in meaning. In his *Note-Books* one finds such entries as: "A German, Karl Kremertartarlau . . . Jews: Rosalia Aromat, Perchik [little pepper] . . . A Czech, Vtichka . . . Russians: Firsikov [comical sound], Sexton Catacombov, Actress Guitarova, Alexey Ivanovich Prokhladitelny [refreshing] or Dushespasitelny [soul saving]; A girl: 'I would like to marry him, but I am afraid of the name — Madame Refreshing!' "[15]

Besides using many literary pseudonyms, he signed letters to friends as "Archpriest Antonius." Writing to his brother Alexander (whom he nicknamed "Gusev" — goose) after the first performance of his play *Ivanov*, he used another amusing signature: "Your Schiller Shakespearovich Goethe."[16]

As a boy, he loved practical jokes and disguises. Once

[14] Chekhov to Morosova (his aunt) , Aug. 27, 1883.
[15] Chekhov, *Note-Books, passim.*
[16] Chekhov to Alexander Chekhov, Nov. 24, 1887.

ANTOSHA CHEKHONTE

he even called in torn clothes on his uncle, who, not recognizing the little beggar, gave him three kopeks. This talent enabled him to satisfy the great passion of his life, the theatre, which attracted him from his earliest days. Attendance at shows of any kind was forbidden by the rules of the Gymnasium. The pupils, for concealment's sake, had to use make-up or false beards if they were to penetrate the wicked temple of the muses. If a boy were caught in the gallery (called "little paradise"), he risked cruel punishment. In the case of the young Chekhovs, punishment would have been doubled, for their father was even stricter than the masters at school. However, Antosha and his brothers were never detected in their theatrical escapades. Under the protection of Anton's masterful disguises, they enjoyed every performance to which they could gain free admission, indifferent as to whether the play was operetta, comedy, or drama, so long as it was theatre. They would come early, wait for the doors to open and then rush up the stairs, breathless with excitement. Then Antosha would, for weeks afterward, enthusiastically impersonate the characters he had seen, and Nikolay, a gifted musician, would play the music on the piano.

Even if the boys enjoyed most the delightful flavor of forbidden fruit, the importance of those early impressions cannot be disregarded. Dramatic art has always been the highest expression of the artistic nature of the Russians and the actors looked upon the practice of their profession as an enlightening mission. Occasionally Antosha would meet an actor, and then the topic of their conversation would invariably be the theatre. These were stimulating experiences for the gifted boy, whose taste was rapidly forming. They left their mark on his unique personality. Young as he was, "Chekhonte" soon showed a decided aversion to any kind of cliché or affectation. Simplicity seemed to him the only possible manifestation of art.

He saw majestic simplicity around him in nature — the steppe — and in its vast monotony he felt the very breath of the unsophisticated Old Russia. Beautiful, colorful memories were ever attached to the journeys he made in his childhood across the steppe on visits to his grand-father, who lived in the province of the Cossacks of the Don. The long trip in a cart, camps by the fire, the wide expanse of land devoid of any romantic, startling scenery — all appealed to the natural sobriety of his mind, filled his young soul with a strange happiness, and gave him a divine sensation of freedom.

The grandfather, Iegor Mikhailovich, struck the future author as a much stronger personality than his own father. Originally a serf, the older Chekhov had, through incessant work, succeeded (1841) in buying his freedom for 3,500 rubles, and during Anton's childhood he had come to be supervisor of the large property of Count Platov, the hero of the Napoleonic War of 1812. The boys loved to visit Iegor Mikhailovich because he was a kindly man. Yet he made them work hard, considering it the duty of everyone to work. Many years later Chekhov wrote to Suvorin (August 29, 1888): "In my childhood, living at my grandfather's on the property of Count Platov, I had to work from dawn to dusk."

We may readily assume that in the early memories of Chekhov there were just two bright spots — the theatre and the steppe — two factors which played an overwhelming part in his further development.

III

Exodus

TAGANROG, on the sea of Azov, had once been a considerable center for Southern Russia but, with the gradual filling up of the harbor, it lost its significance and became just another uninteresting, sleepy town. Yet the Chekhovs liked it; it was their home. Anton Pavlovich always remembered with pleasure its tiny houses, its lime trees, and especially the surrounding steppe, which made an abiding impression on his mind, much as the landscape of Normandy left its mark on Maupassant, with whom later on he was so often compared.

When a railroad was built to Rostov (two hours distant) and failed to touch Taganrog, the town lost its last shred of importance. Pavel Iegorovich's business, never prosperous, rapidly declined. His love for the lives of the saints and for church music had taken too much time. The final catastrophe, though long expected, caused great consternation. House and furniture were sold at auction, and Chekhov's parents went to Moscow, where their two older sons, Alexander and Nikolay, were continuing their studies.

This event happened in 1876. Antosha, a boy of sixteen, was left alone in Taganrog, without means of subsistence. It was the first and the last separation. One can

easily imagine how he missed Masha, his sister and devoted confidante, and especially his kind mother. In a
letter to a cousin, M. M. Chekhov (May 10, 1887), he
asks him to stand by her since she was "broken in health
and in morale." However, letters from that period of
Antosha's life are scarce; only a few facts about him are
known.

He was tutor to a young Cossack, Kravtsov, a nephew
of the merchant, Selivanov, who had bought the Chekhov
house. The two boys spent the summer riding horseback
through the country — "a fantastic land" Anton later
called it. The nights under a velvety sky covered with
myriads of stars, the chill of the mornings, the sunrise,
the birds, the colors, the fragrances, the vast horizons
molded the soul of the young boy and are beautifully
recorded in "The Steppe" (1888), the story with which
Chekhov's fame began.

That peaceful, idyllic existence was soon to terminate.
Fate had endowed Anton with many gifts, but from the
beginning it withheld from him a most precious treasure
— health. A bath in icy water after a long walk on a hot
day resulted in a serious illness, which lowered his resistance and permanently weakened him, thus facilitating
the development of the dread disease which was to bring
him so early to his grave. All his life, Chekhov was to
remember that hot summer day of 1877: "Once on the
road, I was taken ill and spent a night of agony in an
inn."[17] The inn, the friendly innkeeper and his wife, who
took care of Anton, are masterfully portrayed in "The
Steppe."

A kind German, Doctor Strümpf, treated him at the

[17] Chekhov to Pleshcheyev, Feb. 9, 1888. Alexey Nikolaevich Pleshcheyev
(1825-1893) a distinguished Russian poet, editor of the literary section of
the *Sieverny Viestnik* (Messenger of the North).

beginning of this cycle of suffering and sorrow, which was to close twenty-seven years later in the Schwarzwald with another German physician, Doctor Schwöhrer, in attendance. Chekhov recovered from his first illness, made friends with the doctor, and dimly, in his subconscious mind, came to the decision that he would become a physician himself.

Meanwhile he continued at the Gymnasium. Free of his father's tyranny and the necessity of spending his time in the grocery store, he became a much better student. Even in Greek, which he loathed, his marks were higher. Latin and religion remained, however, his favorite subjects. Cherished by Father Pokrovsky for his endless knowledge of Scripture, "Chekhonte" began to write compositions that showed evidences of literary talent. The long prayers he had learned in his early childhood and the reading in the *Chetyi Minei* had given him a large vocabulary of the purest Russian and that feeling for the Russian word which underlay, in his later years, the graceful lightness of his style.

Many of his stories, such as "The Bishop," "The Student," and "Happiness," illustrate how deeply he sensed the beauty of his mother tongue. And "Holy Night," an exquisite tale, could have been written only by one who stood close to the source of the delightful old language. In his mature years, as a famous writer speaking to younger contemporaries, he always emphasized the importance of that fluent simplicity which became almost ethereal in the musical cadence of *The Cherry Garden*.[18]

Chekhov's literary tendencies developed rapidly in these years of independence and precocious maturity. Books

[18] Erroneously translated as *The Cherry Orchard*. Chekhov entitled his last play *Vishnevy Sad*, which means *The Cherry Garden*. It was meant symbolically. The Student Trofimov, before he leaves the house forever says: "All Russia is our Garden."

and the theatre occupied his leisure. Spielhagen, Victor Hugo, Cervantes aroused his enthusiasm. In a letter to his younger brother Mikhail (July, 1876), Anton advised him to read *Don Quixote* and to recommend it to "the brothers," if they did not already know it. "So Madame Beecher Stowe has pressed tears from your eyes," the sixteen-year-old critic added. "Well, I read her myself, once upon a time. About six months ago I read her again for experimental reasons, and afterwards I had the disagreeable feeling one gets from eating too many raisins or currants."

This growing taste in literature did not, however, prevent Anton from reading comic magazines with pleasure, nor from enjoying funny stories as much as ever. Drossi, a contemporary of Chekhov at the Gymnasium, relates: "Along with Bocle and Schopenhauer, whom we read as a matter of duty, we also eagerly devoured comic magazines, *Budil'nik* [The Alarm Clock], *Strekosa* [The Dragonfly], and others. On Sundays and holidays we met early at the public library and, forgetting our dinner, read those magazines for hours, sometimes bursting into such boisterous laughter that we provoked indignant hisses from the other readers there."[19]

Under Anton's leadership a group of young booklovers at the Gymnasium decided to start a magazine. It was called *Zaïka* (The Stutterer), an altogether suitable name. Anton went further on his own account and produced a drama — *Fatherless*. One cannot help wondering whether the sad memories of his early childhood may not have inspired that particular title. In any event, *Fatherless* was followed by a vaudeville sketch which Chekhov later destroyed. It was called *Not in Vain Sang the Hen*, a title

[19] Feider, p. 9.

n which one senses already the Chekhonte of the gay
student years.

While literature passionately attracted Chekhov, he remained quite indifferent to social questions and never
at this time or later did he join any political group.
Profoundly alien to mere rhetoric, he found standardized
theories repulsive to his broad scientific mind. Years later
he wrote to a friend: "People who are united by opinions
or by a common cause condemn free and broad thought,
especially if they are unimaginative and unintelligent."[20]
When, imitating the grownups, the boys at the Gymnasium
would discuss the revolutionary movements of the '70s or
debate grave problems of social injustice, Chekhov would
placidly remark that he wanted to marry, thus shocking
his idealistic friends with his lack of civic consciousness.

Following on the nihilism and the deliberate dissolute-
ness, the systematic cultivation of rudeness, bad manners,
and bad taste that prevailed in the '60s, a new movement
materialized on the '70s; *populism* became the order of the
day. That was a sentimental epoch and a naïve idealiza-
tion of the peasant came into vogue.

The intelligentsia broke with the upper classes and
their artificial civilization, turned to the peasantry and
saw their only salvation in fusion with the people. But
on closer contact it became apparent that the union which
they so sincerely desired was impossible because of the
utter stupidity of the peasant. Therefore, according to
the well-known radical leader, Lavrov, the sacred duty of
any cultured person was to fight for "general progress" in
order to raise the cultural level of the lower classes, urban
as well as rural.

In company with another famous leader, the sociologist
Mikhailovsky, Lavrov strove to develop in society a deeper

[20] Chekhov to Pleshcheyev, Jan. 23, 1888.

sense of civic responsibility towards "the less fortunat
brother." Accomplished theorists, the two men disregarde
the practical side of life and developed their new ideas i
the domain of the abstract.

Many young followers of Lavrov and Mikhailovsk
were animated by too much zeal in their flirtation wit
the lower classes and went to extremes, as so often hap
pened in Russia. They claimed that the peasants wer
possessors of some unknown truth and, therefore, disdair
ing outward conventionalities, they merged completel
with the people, adopting peasant customs, speech, an
dress. So began the new era of "affected simplicity
(*Oproshchenie*), distasteful to Chekhov. He had "peasar
blood in his veins" and he had never been "startled b
peasant virtues."[21] He failed to see how the low standard
of peasant living, their filthiness, uncouthness, and stu
pidity, could fill anyone with enthusiasm. For his part, h
always loved "intelligent, neurotic people [as opposed t
the stolid peasant], politeness, wit."

Brought up in the grocery store, surrounded by a coars
ness which repelled him, and therefore suffering from th
exaggerated sensitiveness of the true plebeian, he ardentl
desired to rise above his milieu, a fact strikingly illu
trated in a letter to Suvorin (January 7, 1889), the onl
man to whom Chekhov opened his heart: "Besides taler
one must have a certain maturity, a feeling of persona
freedom. . . . Write a story about a young man, a so
of a serf, a former grocer, a choir boy, a student of th
Gymnasium and the University, who was brought up o
respect for rank, on kissing the hands of priests, on servi
ity; who gave thanks for every morsel of bread he at
was whipped many times, went to his tutoring in galoshe
[perhaps because he had no shoes], tortured animals, love

[21] Chekhov to Suvorin, March 27, 1894.

to dine at the houses of rich relatives, and was a hypocrite before God and men through realizing his own nonentity! Do write how this young man squeezing the slavery out of his system drop by drop, awakes one morning and feels that in his veins runs no longer the blood of a serf but the blood of a real human being."

In his endeavor to emerge from the petty surroundings of his youth, Chekhov often thought that money offered the only way to freedom. "There is nothing I desire more," he wrote to Suvorin, October 16, 1891, "than to win two hundred thousand rubles, because there is nothing I love so much as my freedom." And again on November 22, he cried: "Freedom! Freedom!" The long desired freedom came, but only to the dying Chekhov when, deeply wounded by life, he accepted its beautiful but "autumnal" roses with smiling indifference. At the Gymnasium, full of happy anticipation, with wings not yet broken, with arms outstretched towards the rising sun, he greeted his future like the student Trofimov in *The Cherry Garden* and hoped for his share of happiness and blessings. Indeed, it seemed bound to come either through marriage or through unexpected riches!

At that time, however, there were no definite plans in the head of the gay Antosha Chekhonte, who, like any boy of his age, simply believed in his lucky star. He was young and carefree as he started his journey to Moscow, where life was *going* to be, *had* to be, a pleasant, a thrilling adventure.

Moscow before the war, the second capital — nay, the "very heart of Russia" — was a large, odd city. Its winding streets and irregular squares gave it the appearance of a straggling, wide-spreading village, where tiny log houses, remnants of a long-forgotten past, rendered the luxurious palaces more striking. Hundreds of churches — "forty times forty" — filled its frosty air with the golden ringing of their many bells. Cathedrals of bizarre shape, each with its five domes sparkling in the sun, blended harmoniously with the age-old walls of the Kremlin. In the business center, adjoining the Gate of Voskresensk, stood the sacred Iversky Chapel (1669). There, in a Byzantine painting covered with precious stones, glittering in the light of candles, the Mother of God, the most blessed Virgin Mary, bent an emaciated, sorrowful face towards fervent believers. Ardent prayers and ancient chants mingled with the curling clouds of incense, strangely contrasting with the bubbling life outside. Gay restaurants filled with an idle élite that sat listening to languid gypsy songs floating in the air, luxurious shops famous for furs and jewelry, art galleries, theatres with excellent music and world-famous ballet made the city the meeting place of East and West. And if in its peculiar harum-scarum it seemed barbaric to the eyes of the Westerner, it was nevertheless individual and beautiful.

Rich, hospitable, a little *frondeuse*, old Mother Moscow was the center of artistic activity even in the gray and melancholy '80s, and in that respect was inclined to look down upon her younger rival, St. Petersburg. At Moscow, multimillionaire businessmen and the proud ancient nobility, though widely separated socially, met on one common ground, love of beauty. When Russia came out of the strange twilight that had, for decades, prevailed in all phases of her national life, Moscow was the first to awaken from that peculiar lethargy and give new impetus to all expressions of art.

In August, 1879, Chekhov arrived in Moscow. The city which later became so dear to his heart did not appeal to him at all during the first difficult years. In September, 1888, he wrote to his friend, the poet Pleshcheyev: "Moscow seems dreadful to me. Winter has not even begun, yet I am already thinking of summer."

Anton found his family in great poverty. The rapidly aging Pavel Iegorovich had accepted a minor position in the store of the merchant Gavrilov — the "Kingdom of Darkness" that Chekhov describes in his autobiographical "Three Years" (the phrase belongs, however, to A. Ostrovsky, whose plays deal exclusively with mercantile circles). The old man slaved the whole week and could see his wife and children only on Sundays. Life was decidedly not a pleasant adventure. From the very beginning it showed a stern face to the boy of nineteen who, though he had two older brothers, had shouldered voluntarily the heavy burden of supporting the family.

A masterful improvisator from his early childhood and a keen observer of life, Antosha naturally turned to literature in his endeavor to meet these serious financial demands. The October number of *The Dragonfly* contains a story by Chekhov, "Letter of a Landowner of the Province of the Don to his Learned Neighbor." It is a very short affair. Its prototype may be recognized in a letter from his grandfather to his father, in which clumsiness of expression is amusingly combined with the grand style in a truly Chekhovian humor. This, as he used to say, was the beginning of six years of vagabonding through the small magazines" and, in fact, between 1881 and 1888 Chekhov was a contributor to many humorous periodicals — *Strekosa* (The Dragonfly), *Budil'nik* (The Alarm Clock), *Oskolki* (The Glass Splinters), *Sviet i Tieni* (Lights and Shadows), *Zritel'* (The Spectator), *Mirskoi Tolk* (Rumor), etc., signing himself now as "My Brother's Brother," now as "The Man without Spleen," now as "Baldastov" [blockhead]. Destined to be most famous of all was "Antosha Chekhonte."

In an obituary of Chekhov, printed July 4, 1904, two days after his death, his friend Suvorin gave an account of his first efforts: "He began to write at the University. His parents had younger sons and a daughter and lived very poorly. He was distressed that on his mother's saint's day they had not enough money to buy her a cake. He wrote a story, the story was printed, and with the few rubles he earned, they celebrated his mother's saint's day. From that time on he became a provider for his family."[22] The anecdote is touching. It recalls a German collection of moral tales to be read by well-behaved children under a Christmas tree. And Suvorin undoubtedly meant well. Unfortunately the story is not true. Life is complex and elusive and is rarely presentable under such schematic forms.

There is reason for surmising that Chekhov first appeared in print during his Gymnasium years, long before the alleged cake episode. As early as 1877, his elder brother Alexander, then a student at the university in Moscow and a contributor to the comic periodical, *The Alarm Clock*, wrote to him: "Send more — but shorter and sharper. The long ones are colorless." And here is Anton Pavlovich's own statement: "I wrote as a bird sings. I would just sit down and write, never thinking how or what about. It would come by itself. I could write an essay, a story, a short play, at any time and without effort. Like a young calf, or a colt left out in the green and bright meadow, I loped, jumped, kicked, waggled, capered comically. I laughed and made others laugh. . . . I felt very gay, and I imagine it was amusing for outsiders to watch me. Sometimes I pick up one of my early stories

[22] Suvorin, "Malen'kie pis'ma" (Short Letters), *Novoe Vremya*, No. 10179, 1904.

now, read it and laugh myself."[23] Writing was in the blood of Anton Pavlovich. It is true that poverty made him write too much and carelessly, and, dissatisfied, he often questioned the quality of his "eruptions." The eruptions were many indeed. Parodies of all kinds, essays on women, treatises on anatomy, physiological notes, humorous advertisements, criticisms, theatrical reviews, comic stories, plays — all forms of humorous writing came with equal ease from Antosha's agile pen.

Even the gods of Olympus were not safe from his malicious wit. The mighty Jupiter became "the flirtatious boss of the celestial chancellery in love with a cow." And Venus — with a trace of his medical studies — was the goddess of beauty . . . and of mercurial treatments." Describing the four seasons for one of the comic magazines, he explained: "In spring young men and women have heart trouble (*affectio cordis*). Treatment: kali bromatum, valerian, ice . . ."[24]

Had someone, at the beginning of Chekhov's literary career shown him the right way, he might have escaped the deplorably poor taste of the low-class comic papers. Yet satire was quite in keeping with his inclinations, for his real element in his youth was humor. In that period (1881-1885) Antosha was quite indifferent to serious questions. He gazed on life about him with a youth's curiosity, he laughed, capered, kicked, and chose the short comic tale as the form which best corresponded to his happy mood.

In his breathless search for the new themes required by the comic periodicals, he hardly had leisure to consider the plausibility of a situation, and buffoonery became his normal literary manner. Bizarre incidents were coupled

[23] Izmailov, p. 162.
[24] Izmailov, p. 132.

with bizarre, amusing names, untranslatable because their humor lies in the play on Russian words. Even in nonsense writing, Chekhov showed a keener craftsmanship than any of his contemporaries. Yet, as time went on, he began to feel the drudgery of work done in such haste. Endowed with innate literary taste, he was anxious not only to be "funny" but also to give literary finish to his writing. In a letter to Leikin (March, 1883) he complains: "To tell you the truth, it is hard to be funny. Sometimes I blurt out things so absurd that I am disgusted afterwards." And to Suvorin he wrote (February 21, 1886): "I am so happy that you have not conditioned my writing for *Novoe Vremya* on the necessity of delivering my manuscripts at a fixed date. Hurry gives me a feeling of carrying a burden. It hampers the work." Years later he recalled the beginning of his literary career without pleasure.

One must, indeed, admit that the circumstances under which the young man lived and wrote were highly unfavorable. His own urgent need of money and the constant demand on him for more stories tempted him, during his student years, to waste his great talent on "Trifles and Baubles" (the title of a short column he wrote) and to consider his writing only a means of support. His ambition to write with greater care and more leisure was for a long time unrealized. His straitened means and the small regard in which the short story was held at that time so increased his natural timidity that he often declared laughingly of his writing that he "would not object to its being printed on the windowsill."[25] Some of his early tales were, in fact, devoid of artistic value; later he excluded them from the first complete edition of his works.

[25] Feider, p. 161.

Most of his time during these difficult years was spent in study at the Medical School at Moscow, which required incessant work of its students. Was it the memory of the kind Doctor Strümpf that impelled Antosha to undertake the long and strenuous study of medicine? In the auto-biographical note written for Doctor Grigorii Ivanovich Rossolimo, Chekhov stated that he "had only a vague idea about universities." Yet he never regretted his choice, since his "acquaintance with natural science kept him on his guard, gave him a real direction in life and helped him avoid many mistakes."[26] Indeed, all his literary activity showed the spirit of true scientific observation.

Although a welcome contributor to many magazines, Chekhov remained very poor. He wrote to his brother Alexander (May 19, 1883): "The hundred rubles I am earning monthly are squandered for the belly, and I have not the means to replace my gray, worn, shabby frock-coat with something less old." It took him a whole year to save enough money for an overcoat. In childlike happiness, he informed Leikin (March 7, 1884): "The tailor brought a new coat! Congratulations!"

In the second year of his life in Moscow, Antosha wrote a drama, another production of his versatile and needy muse. It was a clumsy play, bristling with horse-thieves, shooting, and dangerous women. At the end there was a railroad accident. It seemed, however, the peak of per-fection to the little Mikhail, who, copying it for his brother, felt chills of excitement. The twenty-one-year-old Anton, seeing its effect on Mikhail, was greatly encouraged and took his creation to the famous actress, Yermolova, with the request that she play the feminine role in it. What Madame Yermolova answered Mikhail never

[26] Mikhail Chekhov, *Anton Chekhov i ego sujety* (Anton Chekhov and His Themes), pp. 19-23.

learned, but Anton, upon reaching home, silently tore his drama into small bits.

His short tales were also sometimes returned with mordant criticisms. Success did not come at once. But Chekhonte was young and life was still beautiful.

Gay and witty, always ready for fun, Anton and his gifted brothers attracted many talented young people. Alexander, who had finished his course at the university, was a valued contributor to humorous magazines and lived in a circle of young writers, whom he introduced to his family. Nikolay, a brilliant student of the Academy of Art, also brought home his friends. Two of them, Korovin and Levitan, became famous painters. The beautiful landscapes of Levitan, permeated with his own peculiar sadness, made him very dear to Chekhov.

Of the older generation, only the poet Pal'min visited Antosha, who was, a few years later, to receive many of the celebrities of his time. Pal'min, an unsuccessful poet, was a colorful figure in the Bohemian quarters of Moscow. Tall and thin, he wore a strange black cloak, with unbuttoned flaps swaying in the air like the wings of a bat. A large hat was perched carelessly on a mane of white, untidy hair. While drunk (and that was often) he mourned the failures of his past, but with heart still young, he was a frequent guest in the hospitable home of Chekhov.

Money was scarce in the happy young crowd and, headed by Pal'min, they would go for their honorarium to Kurepin, publisher of *The Alarm Clock* who, strangely enough, was never at home. Sometimes, weary of waiting, they would become indignant and knock furiously on the door. A surprised, sleepy manservant would appear and ask:

"Whom do you want?"

"Kurepin, naturally."

"He left long ago."

"Did he leave any message for us?"

"Oh, yes, he did."

"What did he say?"

"Well, he said: 'Let them come later. I am busy to-day.'"

The other publishers were no better. For his novel *The Tragic Hunt*, which appeared in thirty-three installments, so many that the readers lost the thread of the plot, Chekhov was supposed to receive three rubles per week. Occasionally he sent his little brother Mikhail for the money. The meek patience of the child who sat politely for hours on the edge of his chair would melt the heart of the editor who would finally ask:

"What are you waiting for?"

"Well, sir, for three rubles."

"I do not have them. Perhaps you would like a theatre ticket, or else new trousers. Please go to my tailor So-and-So, and ask for them on my account."[27]

In the early drawings of the gifted Nikolay Chekhov, which were as autobiographical as Anton's writing, one could often recognize the young author who was celebrating with a bottle of wine the rare event of receiving money. Gaiety reigned among these young men while Antosha climbed happily the thorny path of his initiation.

Hard work and many privations had, however, early begun to undermine his health. It was difficult for him, a Southerner, living as he did under unfavorable conditions, to become accustomed to the harsh climate of Moscow. And there, in mist and chill, was to be born his autumnal mood, capricious and frail.

It is obvious that the transition from the provincial

[27] Feider, p. 21.

home town to the stimulating capital provoked in the impressionable youth the nervous instability which always thereafter characterized Chekhov. Now and then we begin to hear a sad undertone. In his immature story, "Useless Victory" (1882), the youthful actor concludes that "everything is gray and monotonous," and in his only novel, *The Tragic Hunt* (1884), one feels already that unfeigned melancholy, which becomes more apparent in his little masterpiece, *On the High Road* (1884).

Na Bol'shoy Dorogie (On the High Road), Anton's first dramatic work, was based on his story "Osen'iu" (In the Fall). Here we see distinctly the birth of that Chekhovian mood (so well rendered by the German word *Stimmung*), which was, a few years later, to permeate all his writing. A drunken nobleman, stumbling in the depths of misfortune, enters an inn on a dark, rainy evening and begs for a glass of vodka, for which he is unable to pay. His misery provokes only noisy laughter and rude remarks from the riff-raff gathered there for shelter. Finally, the newcomer gives the implacable innkeeper his only possession, a golden medallion containing the portrait of a beautiful woman. The hilarity of the guests increases. Suddenly a lady comes in and asks for someone to repair her carriage. It is the same woman whose portrait is locked in the medallion — the former wife of the unfortunate man. Recognizing her husband, she leaves quickly, without a word of sympathy. While the wretched outcast crouches in the corner, trying to hide himself, the onlookers become suddenly compassionate and give him vodka. The tramp, Merik, who, under apparent rudeness has a warm heart, persuades the innkeeper to return the medallion.

All the characters are depicted with that artistic impassivity that dominated Chekhov's later works. This play is a "slice of life," recorded with keen observation of reality, mitigated by a purely Chekhovian touch, the creation of atmosphere: "It was pouring and pouring, and it seemed that there would be no end to this heinous, dark fall." *On the High Road* did not appear until 1914 with the *Note-Books* of Chekhov, having been suppressed by the censor as "gloomy and filthy."[28]

It was Pal'min, the unhappy poet, who in 1882 introduced Chekhov to Nikolay Alexandrovich Leikin, publisher of the humorous magazine, *The Glass Splinters,* in St. Petersburg. Leikin was a noted humorist, who usually wrote about a specific milieu of uneducated but rich Russian merchants. He had achieved considerable success, and to work for him was a step upward for Antosha, whose experiences are recorded in his vast correspondence, which, with the exception of three years in Taganrog, gives minute details of his life. "*The Glass Splinters* is now a most fashionable magazine," he wrote to his brother Alexander (April, 1883) : "It is read everywhere. To write for *The Glass Splinters* means to have a certificate. I have the right to look down on *The Alarm Clock*; from now on I would hardly work anywhere for a nickel." This comparative success permitted the young author to pay more attention to the form and the content of his writing. The student of Chekhov will be interested to read his stories in chronological order and to watch his development and literary progress.[29]

Towards the end of 1884, Chekhov wrote "Pievichka"

[28] Mirsky, *Contemporary Russian Literature,* p. 92.
[29] "Papasha" (Daddy, 1880); "V Vagone" (In the Railroad Coach, 1881); "Barynia" (The Lady, 1882); "Pievchie" (The Singers, 1884); "Pievichka" (The Chorus Girl, 1884); "Unter Prishibeyev" (Sergeant Prishibeyev, 1885); "Myslitel'" (The Thinker, 1885); "Dietvora" (Children, 1886); "Posledniaya Mogikansha" (The Last Female Mohican, 1885).

(The Chorus Girl), which, although somewhat immature, could be considered on a level with his later works. In describing the little prostitute, a theme which would have appealed to Maupassant, Chekhov avoids the bright strokes of the former, subdues the crudity of a risqué situation, and gives us, in delicate water color, a delightful picture of Pasha, the chorus girl. An insignificant government clerk in a fit of generosity presents Pasha with a cheap gold-plated bracelet. His wife, who believes her to be a dangerous siren, comes to Pasha's house and accuses the girl of ruining her and her three children. She requests that Pasha return all the gifts she has ever received from the unfaithful husband. The girl, terrified, surrenders not only the bracelet but all her miserable belongings, while the furious woman insults her for her poverty. Pasha is distressed; she admires "the lady," her slim fingers, her black, angry eyes, her "refined" manners. Left alone, she suddenly realizes that she has been insulted, cries, pities herself, and regrets the loss of her cheap jewelry.

In this story we see another purely Chekhovian trait — his impartiality. He has no more sympathy for Pasha than for the other woman. He merely shows them to us as they are. Though he still loves amusing words and bizarre situations, he has already begun to watch keenly the desperate triviality around him. In 1885 there appeared his story, "Sergeant Prishibeyev," a kind of *Miles gloriosus*, depicting a boastful soldier who, unlike his prototype in Plautus, does not brag about his riches or his love affairs, but, sure of his intellectual superiority, considers himself a paragon and poisons the existence of his neighbors.

More and more Chekhov exposes social wounds and shows a profound understanding of life. The plot of his tales is always simple, reminding one of an etching from a master's hand with all unnecessary details eliminated. One striking example of this artistic economy is the story, "V Sudie" (In Court, 1886) which Tolstoy considered a masterpiece. An old peasant is brought into court for the murder of his wife. The soldier who accompanies the prisoner suddenly stumbles, provoking general laughter at his clumsiness, but the reader may be assured that Chekhov has a definite purpose in mentioning this seemingly unimportant incident. The old peasant denies his crime and turning suddenly to his guard, who is his own son, summons the soldier to testify for him. Attorneys and judges are startled by the strange trick played by life. Although accustomed to tragic situations, these hard men scarcely dare to look at the crimson face of the soldier, who, in accordance with military discipline, remains motionless at his post.

Chekhov, an impressionist, creates a form entirely different from the old literary traditions: "In my opinion the descriptions of nature should be very short and apropos," he wrote to his brother Alexander (May 10, 1886). "Stock phrases, like 'the setting sun, bathing in the waves of a dusky sea, inundated with purple golden rays' and so forth, or 'swallows flying over the surface of the water twittered cheerfully,' these stock phrases should be avoided as a ditch. In the description of nature one has to dwell on particularities, grouping them in such a way that after reading them, on closing his eyes, one could still see the picture. In the sphere of psychology there should also be particularities. But beware of the commonplace. It is best to avoid the description of the mental state; one should try to make it clear through the actions of the heroes."

Often posing as an acknowledged master, he took a childish pleasure in teaching. Inasmuch as the audience was still wanting, he addressed his sermons to his brother Alexander, writing him (April 19, 1883) : "You have a story where a young married couple do nothing else but kiss each other during dinner, snivel, and waste their time in empty talk. There is not one sensible word, only *complacent inanities*. You did not write it for the reader. You wrote it because you liked that babble yourself."

Objective impassivity became Chekhov's definite literary credo. Later he wrote to a friend: "For a chemist there is nothing impure on earth. A writer should be just as objective as a chemist; he ought to know that dungheaps have a very respectable place in the landscape and that evil instincts are just as inherent in life as good ones."[30]

The year 1884 was marked for Chekhov by two important events. He finished his course at the university and "with his doctor's certificate in his pocket" was the happiest man in the world. It was not, however, medicine which attracted him, but literature, "that mistress" from whom he was never more to part.[31] The same year he printed at his own expense *Skazki Mel'pomeny* (Tales of Melpomene) over his usual pseudonym, "Antosha Chekhonte." This collection of his early tales, although the stories were already known to readers through various periodicals, was received with interest.

Chekhov, more encouraged by this success than by his doctor's diploma, went for a summer to Voskresensk, a small town in the province of Moscow, where his brother Ivan was teaching. It was a pleasant little town and Ivan had many friends there. Through him Anton met Colonel Mayevsky and became acquainted with military circles.

[30] Chekhov to Madame Kiseleva, Jan. 14, 1887, after she reproved him for his story "Tina" (The Mud, 1886) .

[31] This was an often-repeated statement of Chekhov. "Literature is my mistress and medicine my lawful wife," he wrote to Suvorin, Sept. 11, 1888.

Many years later, Mayevsky and other army officers appeared in his drama, *The Three Sisters*. The early impressions of Chekhov were often stored in his mind for a long time before they took concrete literary form in his mature work.[32]

At Voskresensk, relatively carefree, he studied life around him attentively. Occasionally he worked in the local hospital, where he observed with keen interest the medical staff and the peasants who came for treatment. Many of them were reflected in his tales, as in a silver mirror.[33]

Though he fully realized the value of medical training, it does not seem that Chekhov derived any particular enjoyment from medical practice, which often bored and annoyed him. Neither did he experience the sharp disillusion in medicine so ably depicted by his younger colleague, Veresaev, in his *Notebook of a Physician* (1895-1900). The attitude of Anton Pavlovich seemed to parallel that of another medical man, Constantine Leontiev, one of the most profound Russian writers. Leontiev highly appreciated his medical training, which developed his sober and logical thinking.[34] He felt indebted to it for his healthy conception of life, for freedom from superstition, but he had had to suppress in himself a sort of revulsion aroused by his first experience with death. In his autobiographical novel, *Home*, Leontiev describes the reactions of the young medical student, Rudnev: "His imagination was painfully struck by corpses, blue, green, thin, swollen by water, strangled; by frozen drunken

[32] "I prefer to write by reminiscence." So Chekhov wrote to Batushkov, professor of French literature in the University of St. Petersburg, Dec. 15, 1897.

[33] "Perpetuum Mobile" (1884); "Mertvoe Tielo" (The Dead Body, 1885); "Vskrytie" (Autopsy, 1885).

[34] Leontiev, *Sobranie sochinenii* (Complete Works), Preface, I, 2.

females, lonely old men and women, whom nobody claimed for burial, and who were cut to pieces by students. . . . He had to live a whole year, struggling with himself to become accustomed to the continuous contemplation of death in all its sordid and bothersome aspects."[35]

It was precisely this "contemplation of death" which was so dreadful to the young Chekhov. For a short time, however, he thought that medicine would remain his "lawful wife." He notified Leikin that his practice was "turning up little by little" (February 16, 1886). Later he wrote to Suvorin (September 11, 1888): "You advise me not to hunt two hares at once, and not even to think about my medical profession. Why not? I feel more cheerful and satisfied when I realize that I have two things to do instead of one."

Perhaps Chekhov might have pursued his two careers together and, while becoming an eminent physician would have remained unnoticed in literature. Who knows? But fate decided differently. His health was failing and it became difficult for the young doctor to live the active life of a medical man. Clouds were slowly gathering over the head of the gay Antosha Chekhonte. He wrote to his school friend, Sergeyenko (December 17, 1884): "I hoped to go to St. Petersburg for the holidays, but was delayed by haemoptysis (not consumptive)." The words in the parentheses speak eloquently for the intelligent young physician who tried hard to believe in his perfect health. "I do not want to be sounded by my colleagues," he confessed to Leikin (April 6, 1886). "What if they should discover something like lengthened breath or altered resonance? I think in my case not my lungs are at fault, but my throat." For thirteen long years, with a strange consistency never displayed elsewhere, Chekhov soothed

[35] Leontiev, *Sobranie sochinenii* (Complete Works), I, 267.

himself by interpreting according to his own wishes the menacing symptoms of his illness. He wrote to Suvorin (October 14, 1888) : "I cough every winter, fall, and spring, and on wet summer days . . . But tuberculosis or other serious lung troubles are recognized only by connected symptoms, which is not my case. If the haemoptysis which occurred in the District Court[36] had been a symptom of the beginning of tuberculosis, I should already have been in the Beyond. Such is my logic." It was a strange "logic" indeed. Like the proverbial ostrich hiding its head in the sand, he pretended not to see the approaching enemy. No one would have recognized the sturdy little boy with chubby face in the tall, long-limbed young man, slender and frail. How his family could so strangely disregard the state of his health remains incomprehensible.

The constant need of money made Chekhov ask his friend Leikin for more work and from 1885 on he began to send his stories also to the *Peterburgskaya Gazeta* (Petersburg Gazette) , a widely read daily newspaper, which introduced the young author to a large circle of serious readers. It was a new conquest, and Chekhov, who had in his early days an extraordinary capacity for joy, was once more in high spirits. The summer came, and with it an apparent recovery in health. He had never felt so well; life seemed again to be "unspeakably beautiful." For his vacation he rented a house in Babkino, the property of the rich landowner, Kiselev, whom he had met the previous year. The Kiselevs belonged to society. They received the young doctor with the graciousness of people of the world, and soon a real friendship developed between them. Madame Kiseleva, a lively and educated woman, was especially pleased to discuss literary themes

[36] In November and December, 1885, Chekhov as a correspondent for the *Petersburg Gazette* attended several trials in the Court.

with Chekhov. The children also liked the gay young man who told them so many interesting stories. For his part, he watched the youngsters with keen interest and his most charming tales about children can be traced to the young Kiselevs.[37]

The residents of Babkino always spent their evenings together. Soon the young doctor became a general favorite. His witty anecdotes amused everybody and were invariably acclaimed. The experience reminded him of the bygone days in Taganrog Classical Gymnasium. He remembered his "funny book," the noisy gaiety of the boys and the roars of laughter in the teachers' quarters. Success is always encouraging, and the happiness of Anton Pavlovich during that pleasant summer was complete.

The news spread rapidly that Babkino was about the jolliest place in the world, its hosts and their friends most charming. Many young people from the neighborhood came to join them. A frequent visitor was the painter, Levitan (1861-1900), who lived near by. He was tall, dark, handsome, and was always involved in tragic love affairs. He used to attempt suicide at regular intervals and this gesture, to his secret delight, created for him among the ladies the reputation of a dangerous man, to be handled with special care.

A few years later, in the story "Poprygun'ia" (The Flippant, 1892) Chekhov represented Levitan as a rather dubious character, thus beginning their estrangement. While they were at Babkino, however, their friendship was sincere, and, in the company of the gay and natural Anton Pavlovich, Levitan dropped his Byronic pose. The two young men displayed boundless capacity for amusing

---

[37] "Kukharka Zhenitsia" (The Cook's Wedding, 1885); "Doma" (At Home, 1885); "Zhiteyskia Melochi" (Trifles, 1886); "Grisha" (1886); "Dietvora" (Children, 1886); "Mal'chiki" (The Boys, 1887).

improvisations, as Izmailov, Chekhov's biographer, tells us. One especially met with general success: attired like Bedouins, with turbans on their heads, their faces turned towards the East, they would invoke the great Allah and his Prophet; then they would quarrel, fight, and finally, dying, would entrust their souls to Asrael, the Angel of Death; soon the two Arabs would be lying on the lawn of Babkino, to the delight of the children, who felt that they were witnessing the marvels of *The Thousand and One Nights*.

Besides possessing a large library, the Kiselevs received numerous newspapers and magazines, which the family and their guests read together. Often differing opinions provoked long, truly Russian discussions, interspersed with music or picnics. Chekhov felt the charm of that pleasant life, so strikingly in contrast with his own. It was as though he had entered a colorful new world. Most stimulating of all, perhaps, was Begichev, the father of Madame Kiseleva. A former Director of the Imperial Theatre and a great lover of art, widely read, well-mannered, the old man contributed much to the aesthetic and worldly development of Chekhov.[38]

Babkino, with beautiful surroundings and interesting friends, stimulated tremendously the literary activity of Anton Pavlovich. Medicine was almost forgotten; it seemed to be out of harmony with the note of general idleness. The young doctor confessed to Leikin that patients bored him. Literature alone was the center of his world. With youthful ecstasy, he felt that he was drawing from life unknown vigor and inspiration. Playfully, in two hours, between plunges in the swimming pool, he

[38] Under the influence of the talks with Begichev, Chekhov wrote "Vied'ma" (The Witch, 1886); "Agafia" (1886); "Nedobroe Dielo" (Evil Deed, 1887); "Volodia" (1887).

scribbled his delightful story, "Yeger'" (The Huntsman, 1885), and sent it to the *Petersburg Gazette*. He probably would not have been so lighthearted if he had known that this particular tale would mark the turning point of his career. "The Huntsman," although inspired by Turgenev's "Meeting" (in *A Sportsman's Sketches*), was, nevertheless, so new and charming that it met with enthusiasm in the editorial office of the *Petersburg Gazette*. Imbued with sunshine and fresh air, written under the fortunate circumstances of good health and peace of mind, it stands by itself and forms a harmonious final chord in the works of Antosha Chekhonte. It is a beautiful painting in warm, rich colors, a bright summer day, the only one in the gloom that surrounds this minstrel of autumnal moods. The story tells us that it is noon. The huntsman Iegor walks leisurely, enjoying this beautiful world, meets by chance his wife, Pelageya, whom he had left long ago. The woman begs him to return to their home, but Iegor is a vagabond, a dreamer. He loves his freedom, his gun, the wide fields and forests. No, he will not go back to the stifling peasant life, to this stupid woman. Straight, handsome, indifferent, this modern Nimrod departs, and soon his red shirt merges with the "golden sea of ripened rye."

The veteran writer Grigorovich, and other collaborators of the *Gazette*, acquainted with the short stories of Antosha Chekhonte, were delighted and intrigued at the same time. Who was this mysterious young man who wrote so beautifully? Why was he using that strange pseudonym? The mischievous Leikin, who remained silent for a while, finally declared: "Friends, I discovered a new Shchedrin."[39] Later he boasted: "I gave birth to

[39] Mikhail Evgrafovich Saltykov (1826-1889), better known under the pseudonym Shchedrin, was a famous Russian satirist.

Chekhov!" Grigorovich was in ecstasy. It was his particular avocation to patronize newcomers in Russian literature. Forty years before he had introduced the struggling Dostoyevsky to Nekrasov, who published *The Poor People* in his magazine (*Peterburgskii Sbornik*). This first novel made Dostoyevsky famous overnight. Now Grigorovich rushed to Suvorin, the influential publisher of *Novoe Vremya* (New Times), and said: "Alexey Sergeevich, do invite Chekhov [to collaborate in *Novoe Vremya*]; read his 'Huntsman.' It would be a sin not to invite him." Suvorin, impressed by the excitement of his friend, wrote to Kurepin, publisher of *The Alarm Clock*, and asked him to extend his invitation to Chekhov. Kurepin sent for the young man and transmitted the flattering invitation, which he supplemented with fatherly admonition and advice. Chekhov listened with a twinkle in his eye, remembering the shoes he had worn out trying to collect his honorarium, smiled, and started gaily on his journey to St. Petersburg.

In her *Recollections*, Madame Suvorina relates how enthusiastically Grigorovich spoke to her about his new protege. "What a talent, my dear soul [*doushechka*], very young indeed, but one already feels in him a genuine man of letters."

One cannot sufficiently emphasize what establishing his connection with Suvorin meant for Chekhov. It developed soon into the deepest, and perhaps the only, friendship in his life. It marked a new era in his literary career and brought him general recognition.

In an amusing letter to his brother Mikhail (December, 1885) Anton Pavlovich described his first meeting with Suvorin: "After having taken my furnished room in Oleinichkov's house, I washed and put on a new coat, trousers, and pointed shoes. First I went to the *Peters-*

burg Gazette, and from there to *Novoe Vremya* where I was received by Suvorin. He was very courteous and even shook hands with me. 'Do your best, young man,' he said. 'I am satisfied with you, only go to church often, and do not drink vodka. Breathe at me!'[40] I did. Suvorin, not noticing any vodka odor, turned and called 'Boy!' A boy appeared and was ordered to bring tea and a few lumps of sugar. After this the respectable Mr. Suvorin gave me money and said: 'One has to be careful with money. Pull up your trousers!' "

[40] Chekhov used that incident in his story "Three Years (1895)."

Chekhov and Suvorin

ALEXEY SERGEEVICH SUVORIN (1834-1912) was
an important figure in the history of Russian journalism.
His father, a simple peasant, had taken part in the famous
battle of Borodino (1812), and had seen Napoleon and
the *Grande Armée*. Because of that fact, many of those
who knew Alexey Sergeevich considered him as old as the
walls of the Kremlin; he seemed to link the present with
that long-forgotten past.

Suvorin received a military education, but, after a time,
resigned from the army and became a schoolmaster.
Gifted and ambitious, he soon realized that life in the
provinces would hamper his plans for wider development.
He decided to move to the capital, and, in 1861, too poor
to pay for transportation, traveled on foot to Moscow,
where he became a contributor to various periodicals. In
1863, at the instigation of Countess Salias de Tournemir
(better known in Russian letters under the name of
Evgenia Tour), Suvorin went to St. Petersburg, where
he soon became a leading journalist. In 1876, he founded
the most widely circulated daily paper in Russia, *Novoe
Vremya* (New Times), essentially a pro-government
organ, serving for the most part the ideals of militant
Russian nationalism and anti-Semitism. Yet, liberal in his

own fashion, Suvorin used to print in his paper articles presenting different political points of view and his own *Short Letters on Various Questions.* Jokingly he called *Novoe Vremya* a parliament, while the satirist Saltykov (Shchedrin) nicknamed it "As you desire, Sir!" in mockery of its supposed servility.

Besides his newspaper, which was an immensely successful enterprise, Suvorin founded a publishing house and developed a wide sale for inexpensive books. A great lover and connoisseur of the theatre, he stood at the head of the literary and artistic group of St. Petersburg and wrote excellent theatrical critiques. Finally, in 1895, he founded the Little Theatre, which introduced the plays of Ibsen and Hauptmann and his own drama, *Tatiana Riepina,* to the Russian public.

Courageous and energetic, he created out of nothing an immense fortune, had wide and influential contacts, and was a self-made man after the American fashion. His diary, published in 1923 (Moscow), has great interest for the reader of today. It discloses two new aspects of his character, his biting sarcasm and his independent political opinions.

His brilliant mind and keen artistic discernment led him naturally to guide and to protect the talented young author. It has already been noted that the contact with *Novoe Vremya* had enormous moral and material significance for Chekhov. From Suvorin's diary we learn how strong was the bond of friendship between these two gifted men during many years. Both sons of serfs, both endowed with unusual intelligence, they were powerfully drawn to each other despite the difference of twenty-six years in their ages. In his numerous letters to Suvorin, Chekhov cast aside his usual timid reticence and poured out his soul, remembering that the old man himself knew only too well the hardship and the bitterness of life. The complex nature of Chekhov could never be fully understood without those letters, which reflect all the phases of his existence. They are human documents of great interest in which every subject, from everyday occurrences to philosophical speculation, is discussed.

Chekhov made his first appearance in *Novoe Vremya* with a beautiful story, "Panikhida" (Mass for the Dead).[41]

A shopkeeper, Andrey Andreevich, comes to the church to pray for his daughter, an actress, who has just died. He wants to have a Mass said "for the harlot Mary" and is completely unaware of the reasons for Father Grigory's indignation at this phrase. "Tell me, Andrey Andreevich, did you write this?" And the old priest hands him the scribble with the shocking word. "Such language here in the house of God! Just tell me," continues the priest in an angry whisper, "what have you on your shoulders? A head or some other object?"

The shopkeeper is speechless with surprise. He thought he had done well in pointing out to the Almighty the fact that his daughter was not quite a lady, but an actress, an actress, mind you. He himself had been slightly ashamed of her when, on rare occasions, she spent a few days with him. In vain the priest tries to explain that she was famous, that her death was mourned by many. He cannot understand, and yet his heart is heavy. He remembers his little Mary, that sweet blonde girl, too slender to be well, "with eyes as large as copper coins." He remembers her tears on her last visit, her sad words: "How magnificent this place is! Oh, Lord! how beautiful is my native land." And "she cried, breathing heavily, as if she knew that she had not very long to live." And

[41] *Novoe Vremya*, No. 3581, 1886.

Chekhov had already acquired this same dreadful knowledge about his state. Into the last words of Mary, he put his own sorrow, his love of nature and his fear of an early death. The feeling of fitness and health after the happy summer in Babkino could not last through the cold winter of Moscow; the hope of complete recovery had to be given up. "I am ill . . . haemoptysis . . . weakness . . . It would be advisable to go south but I have no money," he confessed to Leikin (April 6, 1886). To his friend, Madame Kiseleva, the charming hostess of Babkino, he wrote (September 25, 1886) with humorous sadness: "I am always ailing, and am turning little by little into a mummified dragonfly."

Not capable of rebellion, but caught in the spider web of conflicting thoughts, he brooded over the passing hours, the mystery of the eternal night, and life itself, which "does not end with reward for all the suffering, nor with apotheosis, but death."[42] Thus, the gentle soul of Chekhov was slipping into profound despair, into the land of weird dreams and shadows. He lived henceforth in an odd drowsiness which paralyzed his actions, his will. Strange destiny! Increasing fame and vanishing happiness, which he had left, it seemed, in *The Glass Splinters*, *The Alarm Clock*, and *The Dragonfly*. From now on the *leit-motif* of all his writing was to be misunderstanding and sorrow; the pinpricks of everyday existence were transformed into the unseen tragedy of life.[43]

The "Mass for the Dead" was signed, as usual, "Chek-

[42] "Palata No. 6" (Ward No. 6), Marks edition of Chekhov's works, VIII, 174.

[43] It is interesting to note that consumptive people appear in many of Chekhov's tales: "Tsviety Zapozdalye" (Late Flowers); *Ivanov;* "Nievesta" (The Betrothed); "Gusev"; "Uchitel'" (The School Master); "Razskaz Neizvestnago Cheloveka" (The Tale of the Unknown Man); "Chiorny Monakh" (The Black Monk). As for the physicians, we meet them in almost every story.

honte." Anton Pavlovich, who had lived until then in the company of Leikins and Kurepins, had never received any real recognition, and had developed the habit of considering his talent insignificant. Great was his surprise when *Novoe Vremya* wired for permission to sign his real name to the story. "I gave permission," said Chekhov, "but I confess I was sorry about it; I intended to do some writing for medical papers, and wished to keep my name for serious articles."[44]

What Suvorin wrote to Chekhov about the "Mass for the Dead" we do not know, since Suvorin's letters have not been found, but here is the answer of Chekhov (February 21, 1886): "I thank you for the flattering comment on my work and for the quick printing of my story. How refreshing and even inspiring for my authorship was the kind attention of such an experienced and talented man as you are . . . I fully share your opinion about the end of my story, which was taken out, and thank you for your constructive remarks. I have been writing for six years, but you are the first to take the trouble to give me not only directions, but also reasons."

The unspoiled young man was soon to be greatly pleased with another letter of recognition, this from Dimitrii Ivanovich Grigorovich (1822-1899), who appeared to him like a *deus ex machina*. Grigorovich was a well-established novelist. His works were, however, too permeated with sentimental philanthropy to be truly artistic, and his place in Russian literature is due rather to the sense of values which he showed in appreciating budding authors than to his own writing. Upon reading "Mass for the Dead," "The Witch," and "Agafia," three exquisite tales printed on Saturdays from February to March, 1886, in *Novoe Vremya*, Grigorovich, who had silently watched Chekhov,

[44] Lasarev-Grusinsky's recollections, in Feider, p. 49.

finally wrote him (March 25, 1886). The letter was formal, starting with "Sir," but every sentence in it betrayed interest and affection. He congratulated Anton Pavlovich upon his real gift, advised him to drop hasty writing, to suffer hunger as he himself had done in bygone days, but always "to respect his talent, and to publish only truly finished stories."

The young writer was delighted and flattered by the attention of the old man. In his answer (March 28, 1886), he willingly admitted his sins: "If I have a talent which should be respected, I confess until now I have not respected it." Grigorovich, pleased that his teachings were so readily accepted, expressed a desire to meet him. The meeting took place, and was followed by a tragicomic episode, as if the author of hundreds of humorous tales had tempted a mischievous Providence! Chekhov wrote to Madame Kiseleva (March, 1887): "The old man kissed me on the forehead, embraced me, wept from tenderness, and all those emotions provoked a serious attack of angina pectoris. He suffered terribly, tossed about, moaned. I sat next to him for two and a half hours, cursing my inefficacious medicine."

Chekhov's reputation was established. Leikin published in 1886 his second book, *Piostrie Razskasy* (Parti-Colored Stories), that "disorderly collection of student writing shorn by the censor."[45] They were received most favorably. Tears were sensed beneath the surface laughter. Important periodicals, such as *Russkaya Mysl'* (Russian Thought) and *Russkoe Bogatstvo* (Russian Wealth), noticed their merit and form.

This success of the young author aroused venomous attacks from some of his contemporaries, who, under a display of refined literary taste, were hiding their bitter envy

[45] Chekhov to Grigorovich, March 28, 1886.

of the growing fame of Chekhov. In the *Sieverny Viestnik* (Messenger of the North, June, 1886), the critic Skabichevsky called him a "clown with his empty, ludicrous newspaper chatter, in pursuit of easy money." Skabichevsky ignored the fact that, despite the constant requests of Suvorin, Chekhov, though very poor, always refused to accept on *Novoe Vremya* "a definite, paid position."[46] He cherished his independence and sent in his stories when he pleased. To the end of his days, Chekhov could not forget the insult of those hard and unjust words. Gorky recalled that, shortly before his death, Anton Pavlovich used to say: "Critics remind me of gadflies that disturb horses at the plough. What are they buzzing for? For twenty-five years I have read criticisms of my stories, and have never received one valuable direction, or heard one sensible word. Only once Skabichevsky made an impression on me, when he wrote that I should die drunk in a ditch."[47]

The contemporary "sovereign of thoughts," the sociologist and critic, Nikolay Mikhailovsky, also disliked Chekhov. He reproached him for his indifference to questions of the social order, and deplored his early literary experiences in *Novoe Vremya* and *Oskolki*. Yet he "understood that filth could not stick to him" and besought him in a letter (February 15, 1888) "to do no evil service, but good."

Such grandiloquent words must have been painful to Chekhov, whose aim from his very youth was toward simplicity. We do not know what he answered, but Lasarev-Grusinsky, a contemporary, relates that he defended *Novoe Vremya* with unusual vehemence and refused, out of gratitude to Suvorin, to leave it. Besides, Anton Pavlovich was anxious to keep his personal freedom — "freedom from

[46] Chekhov to Suvorin, Aug. 29, 1888.
[47] Gorky, *Moï Universitety* (My Universities), p. 264.

[57]

violence, superstition, ignorance, and passion."[48] Mikhailovsky answered with a cool note, showing indignation that a young writer should reject his precious advice, even when unsought. Stubbornly he repeated that by the mere fact of having his stories printed in *Novoe Vremya*, Chekhov did "serve the devil indeed."

Russian radical leaders often assumed the attitude of those who hold the only key to knowledge, wisdom, and truth. Accustomed to the worship of their compatriots, they soon became so convinced of their own superiority that they began to disregard the human herd, until their followers, tired of sheeplike obedience, and ready to grasp other new and more fascinating ideas, turned against them and destroyed them in wrath. Mikhailovsky, a brilliant sociologist, a true son of his time, belonged to the category of "repentant noblemen," who dragged through life the fixed idea of *social guilt*. Their only aim was "to wipe out the guilt of their serf-owning ancestors by sacrificing their lives to the people."[49]

Mikhailovsky believed that his task was to spread radical ideas. Like the men of the '40s, he was an idealist and his conceptions of right and justice were very high. But his strong party feeling induced him to make "his literary criticism quite subservient to civic ends."[50] He stubbornly objected to Chekhov, in whose writing he could, even later, detect no value.

Anton Pavlovich was only too well aware of the superficiality of his early tales, "that ballast, written under the pressure of poverty."[51] His *Parti-Colored Stories* (1886), in bringing him recognition and some money, freed him from the despotism of the humorous papers. Yet, even in

[48] Chekhov to Pleshcheyev, April 9, 1889.
[49] Mirsky, *History of Russian Literature*, p. 280.
[50] Mirsky, *History of Russian Literature*, p. 281.
[51] Chekhov to his uncle, M. G. Chekhov, Jan. 18, 1887.

his mature stories, Chekhov never pretended to teach struggling humanity or to solve its problems. He merely followed his artistic bent. His work is pure art, free from political or civic bias.

As yet the slogan of Gustave Flaubert, "Art for Art's sake," had not reached Russia. Maupassant's masterpiece, *La Maison Tellier* (1881), dedicated to Turgenev and later much admired by Tolstoy for its impeccable form, passed unnoticed. Tolstoy, who was undergoing his conversion, stated in his foreword to Maupassant's works that in 1881 he was not interested in stories of that type.[52] The aesthetic influence of Vladimir Soloviev and of Nietzsche, who "was first of all a powerful emancipator from the fetters of civic duties" appeared only in the '90s.[53] Chekhov, in his timid attempt to stimulate a literary revival, felt ill at ease among the intelligentsia, who were caught in the net of political and social tendencies, problems, courses, and directions, and were, ironically enough, devoid of that aesthetic culture which was destined, a decade later, to submerge Russian society. Harassed and tired, Anton Pavlovich confessed (February 22, 1886) to Leikin that "everything is quite sad." With increasing nervousness, he wished to escape the world around him, realizing the burden of his profession. "I would like to take a trip, a sort of world cruise," he wrote, and casually remarked, "By the way, I am coughing."

Overcome by illness and disillusion, he wrote two years later to Suvorin (December 22, 1888), that sometimes he had "fits of hatred," an emotion never known to him before. Always self-controlled, he showed irritation only when accused of indifference towards moral and social questions.

[52] Tolstoy, "Predislovie k sochineniam Mopassana" (Foreword to the Works of Maupassant) in Tolstoy's complete works, XIII, 76.
[53] Mirsky, *Contemporary Russian Literature*, p. 153.

His friend Shcheglov recalled that vexing comments about his lack of faith and of definite direction in life often reached Chekhov, who would answer: "They say anything about me. Sheer nonsense. I am simply human, I like nature, literature, beautiful women, and hate routine and despotism."

"Political despotism?"

"Any kind, in whatever form it may be expressed — in national affairs or in the Editorial Office of *Russian Thought*."[54]

Yet unkind remarks about his "indifference" seriously annoyed Chekhov, especially since he realized that they were true. Only to Suvorin did he confess, as usual, "I continue to grow stupid, idiotic, indifferent, to fade away, and to cough. Is that old age or laziness? I don't know. I do not want to die, nor to live. . . . My soul is drowsy. . . . That indolent state of mind depriving me of desire and will lasts sometimes for months."[55]

This ever-growing drowsiness, however, was caused not only by the bitterness of his personal life, with its progressing illness, but also, to a large extent, by the deplorable taste, discouragement, and gloom that prevailed in that period of Russian life, the period of reaction.

In the last years of Alexander II, in order to put an end to secret revolutionary activity, there was formed a Supreme Executive Committee under the leadership of Count Loris-Melikov, the "Dictator of the Heart," as he used to be called. In his opinion, Russia could overcome the revolutionary movement only by persuading wide circles of cultivated society to work hand in hand with the government.

[54] Shcheglov's recollections, in *Niva*, June, 1905.
[55] From three letters to Suvorin — Nov. 18, 1891; Oct. 24, 1892; and Aug. 18, 1893.

Active and optimistic, Loris-Melikov sincerely hoped that in the relatively liberal reign of Alexander II the long estrangement between the ruling class and the public might be forgotten. But the dreams of the "Dictator of the Heart" never came true. On the eve of the signature of the long-expected reforms, Alexander II was assassinated (March 1, 1881). His death was an irreparable disaster for the *rapprochement* between government and society. The execution of Zheliabov and Sophia Perovskaya, leaders of the *Narodnaya Volya* (Will of the People),[56] responsible for that act, did not put a stop to the revolutionary movement.

The roots of the *Narodnaya Volya* lay deep in the Utopian socialism and the materialism of the '60s. But in order to understand the bubbling subterranean revolutionary activity during the nineteenth century, the rise of the *rasnochintsy*[57] with their bitter class hatred and the *kaiushchiesia dvoriane* (the repentant noblemen) who carried with them their precious feeling of "social guilt" — all of which culminated in the *Narodnaya Volya* — we have to take a step backward. Without such a retreat the Chekhovian period and Chekhov himself would be incomprehensible.

[56] The word "volya" is difficult to translate. It means "will" and "freedom" at the same time. D. S. Mirsky translates it as "will." *Contemporary Russian Literature,* p. 44.

[57] D. S. Mirsky's definition of the word *rasnochintsy* is: "Rasnochintsy (singular rasnochinets) means literally 'men of various classes.' They include all those who, having received an education, had ceased to be members of the lower classes, but not become nobles." *History of Russian Literature,* p. 204.

V

Dreams and Realities

THE divergence between Russian society and the government began in the early part of the nineteenth century. At first the war against Napoleon in 1812 aroused an enthusiasm never before known. No sacrifice seemed great enough for the general patriotic fervor, and Moscow set ablaze by Russian hands was like a tremendous watch fire, a warning to the approaching enemy.

After the return from the Napoleonic Campaigns, however, the gentry began to compare the Russian regime with the new social order of Western Europe. They found the tyranny of the favorite of the hour — Count Arakcheyev — unbearable after the first liberal years. Alexander I, forlorn and melancholy, had long ago forgotten the smiling philosophy of the great Catherine, his grandmother. Long wars, the misfortune of Europe, the sadness of the dawning romanticism cast their shadows over the gentle soul of this most romantic of the Emperors. He had already been shaken on the very first day of his reign by the tragedy of Mikhailovsky Castle where his father, Paul I, universally hated for his insane cruelty, was choked to death by Count Pahlen and General Beningsen (March 12, 1801).

The Moscow fire had for Alexander a mystic significance.

[62]

A fervent Christian, brought up on the monarchic principle of the continuation of divine power on earth,[58] he believed that Russian Emperors were, through Byzantium, the heirs of the Caesars and that Moscow, the third Rome, had a predominant role to play in the destiny of mankind.

Alexander conceived the idea of saving Russia and Europe and initiated the famous *Sainte Alliance*, signed in Paris, September 26, 1815, by Russia, Austria, and Prussia. This act meant a return to theocratic legitimism. The dreams of freedom were fading!

In 1825, on a trip to the Crimea, in the hope of improving his health, Alexander died in Taganrog (November 19), where thirty-five years later was to be born another lonely soul — Chekhov.

The confusion created by this unexpected death of the childless Emperor was tremendous. His direct heir, the Grand Duke Constantine, military governor of Warsaw, who had secretly renounced the throne many years before, took an oath of allegiance (December 8, 1825) to his younger brother Nikolay. Nikolay, for his part, with the troops of the garrison at St. Petersburg, swore fidelity to the Emperor Constantine (December 9, 1825). "And so between the brothers began a struggle hitherto unknown to history, a struggle not for power, but for renunciation."[59]

The army, not understanding the situation, rebelled. This rebellion was no simple mutiny, for it culminated in the famous December Revolt (December 14, 1825) inspired by the nobility, who became the vanguard of political opposition in those years and seized the first opportunity of the short interregnum to limit the power of their absolute ruler. The December Revolt disclosed the bitter con-

[58] *"Rex est mixta persona cum sacerdote."* Figgis, p. 18.
[59] *Russkii biograficheskii slovar'* (Russian Biographical Dictionary), I, 381.

flict between advanced Russian society, imbued with the rationalistic ideas of the French Revolution, and Russian Tsarism, based on the principles of the Byzantine autocracy and the mystical conception of the supreme mission of the emperors.

The prompt suppression of this revolt by Nikolay I, who was convinced of his divine right, only widened the gulf between the government and the nobility. The young Emperor, striking in appearance, gigantic in stature, had from the very beginning inspired fear rather than love. He had neither the gentle disposition nor the liberal education of his elder brother, Alexander. Brought up by a strict German, General Lamsdorff, he exalted military virtues above all others. His efficiency in wiping out the revolt was a challenge to his hostile subjects.

The Decembrists who had organized the "League of Salvation and Happiness" belonged to the highest society. One hundred and twenty-six of them were banished to Siberia and five were sentenced to death. Overwhelmed by this disaster, the nobility withdrew from political life, thereby proving their total unfitness for decisive action. While they were nursing their wounds, there appeared on the Russian horizon a new class of people, a "plebeian intelligentsia" headed by the critic and Westernizer, Vissarion Belinsky, the "furious Vissarion," who, known for his audacity and fighting character, began the dynasty of the *rasnochintsy*.

Although some of them were gifted and educated, the *rasnochintsy* came from the lower strata of society and scorned the ideals of the nobility, which they could neither share nor understand. They began to uproot the traditions of culture, beauty, and polished manners that lingered in the aristocracy like the last glow of the eighteenth century, that graceful period which still breathes a faint fragrance of roses and brings to memory minuets, white wigs, and slender swords. The old world, which had already lost its prestige with the Emperor, was giving way before the rising lower classes.

At that time (1836) a former officer of the Guard, a hussar named P. Y. Chaadaev, produced a remarkable work as a result of his meditation on history. His *Lettres philosophiques*, written in French, although only four in number, were of tremendous significance. They gave a new impetus to the activities of the Westernizers and the Slavophils — the two groups representing an important ideological movement which had always existed in embryonic form. Chaadaev deplored the infirmity of the old traditions. He pointed out that they never had a solid basis in the historical past of Russia but were merely remnants of the disintegrating Byzantine Empire, to which Russia considered herself heir. He made no attempt to disguise his admiration for the West, especially for Roman Catholicism, and he criticized ruthlessly both Russian life and Eastern Church.

The sensation caused by the *Lettres* was tremendous. Society and government were deeply stirred. The fact that Chaadaev was an aristocrat made the situation difficult. He was not guilty of high treason; therefore he was not subject to exile like a Decembrist. Yet his attacks on state and church constituted an offense which could not be disregarded. He was later declared insane and placed under medical care. The monthly periodical, *The Telescope*, where his first letter appeared, was suspended and its editor, Nikolay Nadezhdin, banished for two years to Ust'-Sysol'sk, a small northern town in the province of Vologda.

Cured of politics for a while, the nobility sought consolation in a profound study of German idealistic philosophy, and in the '40s, in intellectual Moscow (not in bureaucratic St. Petersburg) there appeared the "salons," one of the most important features of the time. In these "salons" the aristocratic dilettanti met with the university circles in long debates on literary and philosophical topics. Condemned to a forced inactivity, dissatisfied with its present, Russians of the upper classes were absorbed in abstract questions, a fact which was by no means a blessing in the development of the national character.

At that period, often referred to as the "meditative '40s," the Westernizers and the Slavophils flourished. The Slavophils believed in the traditions of "Old Russia." They saw true Christianity only in the Eastern Church, which they considered to be humiliated and belittled by the monarchy. As for the monarchy itself, they thought its national character had ended with Peter the Great, who had forcibly transplanted western habits and customs and made of his native land an imperfect imitation of Western Europe.

On the other hand the Westernizers,[60] as the name itself shows, were ardent proponents of Western ideas. They believed that the only way to progress lay in complete fusion with the West; they formed a powerful faction and often met in the "salon" of Chaadaev, who became a very popular figure in Moscow. His "lunacy" was short-lived; he never wrote anything more, but his place is certainly most important in the history of that strange land of Russia where the nobility paved the way to revolutions and the hussars philosophized.

Under the Argus eyes of aroused censorship critical thought was apparently paralyzed, but there was a constant turmoil of protest ready to break out at the first opportunity. Eleven years after the *Lettres* of Chaadaev

[60] We may say the first Westernizer was the Boyarin Artamon Matveyev (1625-1682), a statesman in the government of the Tsar Alexey Mikhailovich, father of Peter the Great.

(1847), Alexander Herzen, who occupied a predominant place in the political and literary history of Russia took up his residence in Western Europe. In 1857 he began to publish in London his famous *Bell*. This weekly paper, free to reveal from abroad abuses and wrongs, had a wide, though clandestine, circulation in Russia. Its political influence was so great that it was secretly read by the Emperor himself.

The accession of Alexander II, that gentle pupil of the romantic poet, Zhukovsky, was like a burst of sunshine after a storm. One of Alexander's first official acts was to put an end to the Crimean War (1856). Then he launched a series of reforms, which at first awakened great enthusiasm. This was especially true of the freeing of the serfs (February 19, 1861). It is interesting to note that this act preceded by only two years the emancipation of the slaves in the United States (1863) and that both Emperor Alexander II and Abraham Lincoln were afterwards assassinated.

With the breath of freedom and the relaxation of the censorship, men began to write what had been hidden during years of silence. It was not long before ideas ran ahead of events, and the unbridled *rasnochintsy* were soon thinking of a "Social Utopia," which could be reached only by destruction of the social barriers. Risen from the depths of society and saturated with scientific materialism, they hoped to rebuild contemporary life. Therefore, they set out with much zeal to tear down the old aristocratic culture, considering it as a hindrance to progress.

This new generation, rough in manners, negligent in grooming and speech, disdained the philosophical meditations of the '40s as an idle pastime of the rich. They had no use for beauty and broke with traditional art and literature, accepting only the critic Belinsky (their first leader) and, to some extent, Gogol in his role of satirist. They turned to natural science, which came into vogue through the works of Darwin and Huxley. Fervent partisans of the theory of evolution, the *rasnochintsy* advocated "exact science" (*tochnia nauki*) as the unique basis, the Alpha and Omega, of progress. Anxious to eradicate religious superstition, they attempted to subordinate the spiritual aspects of life to the methods of "exact science." Agnosticism became synonymous with freedom.

It was only natural that, in their endeavor to establish new social forms, they were also interested in economic theories. Nikolay Chernyshevsky (1828-1889), one of the radical leaders of that time, much admired by the new generation, answered every question of economics with great self-confidence. In his dissertation, *On the Relation Between Art and Reality* (1885), he advanced the idea that both science and art should serve social needs. He considered art as superfluous, since it was merely an imperfect imitation of reality. His treatise soon became a manifesto of a new utilitarian movement. His significance, despite the fanaticism and one-sidedness of his thought was great; he laid the foundation of the Russian revolutionary movement.

The second leader was the gifted and puritanical Nikolay Dobrolubov (1836-1861), whose ideals were not happiness and freedom, but an excessive glorification of work. He dismissed Tolstoy and Turgenev as having no utilitarian value, and thus encouraged antiaesthetic tendencies and narrow party feelings.

The third and the most brilliant of the three, Dimitrii Pisarev (1840-1868), represented Russian radical negation. He believed, too, that science alone will modify human life; art should be rejected and literature accepted only as a servant and a popularizer of science. Paradoxically, Pisarev demolished the established authorities, and so irre-sistible a fascination did he have that for a time he de-throned Pushkin, the great national poet, whom he, in youthful exuberance, thoroughly despised.

D. S. Mirsky says: "Victor Shklovsky, one of the most influential critics of to-day, voiced a widespread feeling when he wrote: 'I detest Belinsky [the first leader of the *rasnochintsy*] and all the other (fortunately, unsuccessful) murderers of Russian literature.' "[61]

One must admit that these radical leaders, though nar-row-minded and too self-confident, were unquestionably gifted. Their renown prepared the way for other *rasno-chintsy*. Those who sought progress in the study of nat-ural science formed a group of "thinking realists" (*mysli-ashchie realisty*), thus emphasizing their "advanced" ideas. They were called "nihilists" by their adversaries, an ap-pellation which they readily accepted and which became a designation of a whole generation of Russian radical society. It is interesting to note that this word was not coined by Turgenev (as erroneously thought), but by Nikolay Nadezhdin (1804-1856), editor of *The Telescope*, a brilliant Russian critic and professor at Moscow Uni-versity. As early as 1829, Nadezhdin used the term "nihil-ist" in his sharp polemic articles: the phrase, "swarm of nihilists," appeared in *Viestnik Evropy* (Messenger of Eu-rope, Nos. 1 and 2, 1829).

The nihilists were soon joined by the "repentant noble-men," who suffered deep remorse for their old nobility prerogatives and felt responsible for the condition of Russia. For their redemption they considered coalescence with the lower classes as their sacred duty. The meeting ground of the two groups was zeal for the interests of the people. So in the '70s there was born in Russia the popu-

[61] Mirsky, *History of Russian Literature*, p. 213.

list movement, so distasteful to Chekhov. Beauty and art continued as symbols of aristocratic corruption, while the "unimaginative '70s present a picture of hopeless Philistinism"[62] and mediocrity.

During the '60s Russian literature reached its highest perfection in the writers of the older generation. The outstanding works of that time were *War and Peace, Crime and Punishment,* and *Oblomov.* The public was not, however, interested in them and blindly followed its new leaders. Tolstoy, as always, stood by himself, but neither Dostoyevsky nor Goncharov agreed with the young radicals. Even the responsive Turgenev displayed hostility towards the reign of the *rasnochintsy.* He scarcely hid his irony when, in his novel *On the Eve* (1860), he chose as a prototype of the new man a Bulgarian — Insarov — in order to show that in Russia there was as yet no hero, nothing but small fry. This depressing realization had its significance for the epoch of Chekhov.

Nevertheless Turgenev, with his artistic perspicacity, felt the general atmosphere and strove to adapt himself to the new ideas. In *Fathers and Sons* (1861) he presented Bazarov as a materialist and a skeptic. This character is a young man, sure of himself, active and energetic, who seems to respond to the ideals of those days. And he was a Russian.

The character of Bazarov provoked a storm of indignation. This portrayal of contemporary crudity was considered by the new generation to be a caricature. The novel, though it aroused great interest, satisfied no one. Pisarev alone greeted Bazarov as the embodiment of the new ideals — Bazarov the hero, the fighter for positive knowledge, the strong man who goes his own way and does not bend before the opinion of the crowd.

[63] Ivanov-Rasumnik, p. 179.

Dreams and Realities

When Dostoyevsky returned from Siberia, where he had spent four years in exile, he aroused general enthusiasm by his famous *Memoirs of the House of the Dead* (1863), an account of his prison experiences. The radicals, however, broke with him after he published *Crime and Punishment* (1866). They showed even greater irritation than they had at the appearance of *Fathers and Sons*. The hero — Raskolnikov — is not a strong man like Bazarov, but a neurotic, who, out of sheer hysteria, attempts to undermine the very foundations of society.

Dostoyevsky, a great psychologist, disclosed in his novels the strange moodiness in the character of the Russians and their unfitness to deal with realities. This particular trait had already been expressed by Goncharov in his masterpiece, *Oblomov* (1858), the hero of which may be considered a symbol of the ineffectiveness and the indolence later depicted by Chekhov in his sad and lyrical fashion.

From the '60s on there was a most peculiar situation in Russia, with a mistrustful government looking suspiciously at everyone, and the intelligentsia split into two distinct groups: the skeptics, who sadly observed the events but did not move a finger for better or worse, and the radicals, active and critical, who joined the subterranean revolutionary movement that led to the assassination of Alexander II. This troubled situation grew worse. The breach continued to widen and paralyzed the normal growth of the state. It was as if a melancholy twilight had fallen, that kept Russians from believing in bright, happy days. Chekhov caught the mood of that tragic misunderstanding which became a national trait and which he masterfully depicted in his mature work.

The reinforcement of authority after the death of Alexander II, the strengthening of the power of both church and state — all this brought still greater gloom. The transition from the twenty-six years of the comparatively liberal government of Alexander II to the reactionary policies of Alexander III — a sharp swing of the pendulum — was too abrupt not to be reflected in the minds of the intelligentsia.

About 1886, when Chekhov wrote his first melancholy tales, the new pessimistic outlook of society was already formed. So the gloom of Anton Pavlovich, naturally intensified by his growing illness, reflected many of the elements of his epoch. He lived among the inactive, talkative, dissatisfied intelligentsia, which formed the background of his literary efforts and, as a true physician who diagnoses the disease, he observed stagnation and inertia and gave us a perfect picture of what he saw around him. In his *Note-Books*, where he usually wrote what appeared striking to him, we find this semi-humorous entry: "The new governor made a speech to his clerks. He called the merchants together — another speech. At the annual prize-giving of the secondary school for girls — a speech on true enlightenment. To the representatives of the press — a speech. He called the Jews together: 'Jews, I have summoned you. . . .' A month or two passes — he does nothing. Again he calls the merchants together — a speech. Again the Jews: 'Jews, I have summoned you . . .' He has wearied them all. At last he said to his Chancellor: 'No, this work is too much for me, I shall have to resign.' "[63]

[63] Chekhov, *Note-Books*, p. 11.

BOOK II

Twilight

VI

Ivanov

IN THE drama *Ivanov* Chekhov gave for the first time a finished portrait of the man of the '8os. Many of his contemporaries recognized in the hero their own psychology: the confusion of the soul, the lack of faith and of ideals — the greatest weakness of that generation. "In our writing there is a lack of spirits that intoxicate and subjugate," Chekhov wrote to Suvorin (November 25, 1892). "Tell me sincerely who among my contemporaries between thirty and forty-five has given to the world so much as one drop of alcohol? Are not Korolenko, Nadson, and all the playwrights nowadays producing a sort of lemonade? Did the painting of Repin or Shishkin ever turn your head? It is nice, talented and yet you cannot forget that you want to smoke. . . . It is a sour, flaccid, boring time. Remember that writers whom we call eternal or simply good and who intoxicate us have one very important characteristic. They lead somewhere and call you to join them, and you feel, not with your intelligence but with all your being, that they have a goal. . . . And we! We describe life as it is and further . . . we do not move. We have neither near nor distant aims and our souls are empty. We have no interest in politics, do not believe in revolution, do not admit the existence of God." And Chekhov deplored the "lemonade" of his time and wrote *Ivanov* to "summarize everything that had been said about complaining and lamenting people."[1]

Ivanov was written in a fortnight. Korsh, the owner of a Moscow private theatre where light comedies and vaudeville were given, was acquainted with Chekhov's humorous stories and asked him to write a play. Anton Pavlovich readily accepted this suggestion. He was highly dissatisfied with the stage of his time and expressed this dissatisfaction a few years later through the speeches of his characters: "I despise the modern stage; it is merely the vehicle of convention and prejudices."[2] "A work of art ought to have lofty ideas, it must express eternal truth."[3] And he began to work with interest in the hope of producing something entirely new. "I am writing a drama," he said to Korolenko, "Ivan Ivanovich Ivanov. . . . Do you understand me? There are thousands of Ivanovs. He is a most ordinary man, not a hero at all, and that is precisely what makes it so difficult."[4]

To his brother Alexander he explained (October, 1887) : "For the first time I have written a play. Mistakes there are many. The plot is complex and not bad. The action is developed peacefully and quietly. Only at the end do I give the public a punch in the nose. This play may be bad, yet I have created a type of literary significance."

Ivanov, even more than "Mass for the Dead," brings to a close a chapter in the life of Chekhov. He is about to enter that dim, melancholy, silver-brown world of late autumn, which was to last almost until his end. In giving the sad and hopeless portrayal of Ivanov, Chekhov showed to what extent the nonconformity of dreams and reality

[1] Chekhov to Suvorin, Jan. 7, 1889.
[2] *The Sea Gull,* Act III.
[3] *The Sea Gull,* Act I.
[4] Korolenko, I, 394-395.

could carry his protagonist, making him a selfish hypo-
chondriac and finally wrecking him at the age of thirty-five.

Ivanov is intelligent and well educated. The misfortunes
which have wrung his soul have developed in him one of
the most destructive Russian traits — *the feeling of guilt*,
the realization of futility, as a result of constant brooding.
Hence his diffidence, his self-pity, his lack of sympathy for
other people's sorrow. In his early days his indifference had
been redeemed by good impulses, but with the years he
has lost faith in his ideals, "his soul is overwhelmed with
despair." His wife betrayed his illusions; she only bores
and irritates him. A charming young girl, Sasha, loves and
idealizes him and believes that if he is "dull, cross, bored
and peevish," it is because life has crushed him. "I love
you madly, without you my life can have no meaning, no
happiness" (Sasha, Act II). She wants him to run away to
America, cheering him with a hope of a new beginning.
"Is it the beginning for me of a new life, is it, Sasha? . . .
Oh, my happiness, my joy!" He is drawn to her by the
mirage of possible happiness, yet there is in his soul only
fear and weariness, since "his life has been full of mistakes,
injustice, and stupidity." Although misunderstood, he is a
"fine fellow," but he "has heaped burdens on his back and
it has broken." His complex nature is incompatible with
that of the stupid Doctor L'vov, proud of his "heartless
honesty." He tries to justify himself: "You are mistaken,
Doctor. In each of us there are too many springs, cogs and
wheels." Lack of will power is the greatest defect of Ivanov.
He cannot submit to the unpleasant atmosphere of his
home, yet he has not the strength to break its fetters. Terrible is the scene with his aggressive, unjust wife, whose
only excuse is her illness and her jealousy. After her death
the realization of his guilt drives him to suicide, despite
the beginning of a new love. This suicide is only a logical

consequence, since his analytic mind refuses to find an issue or even a justification for his aimless life.

Produced by Korsh in the fall of 1887, this play aroused extraordinary excitement: "You cannot imagine what it was," Chekhov wrote to his brother Alexander (November 24, 1887). "I already told you that at the first performance there was such an agitation in the public and behind the stage as has never been seen by the prompter who has worked in the theatre for thirty-two years. . . . After the presentation, there appeared in the Moscow *Gazette* a review by Peter Kicheev, who labelled my play as impudent and cynical rubbish. . . . It seems that during November I was a psychopath."

Chekhov often spoke about the "author psychosis": "I felt it when *Ivanov* was given. . . . Those who come behind the scenes to console or congratulate the author do not realize that they see a temporary lunatic who can fall upon them and bite."[5]

The public was puzzled; only light vaudeville was expected from the author of humorous tales. Yet many agreed that the central character represented a symbol of the times. Ivanov wanders among people like a shadow, without faith, without aim. He is a "superfluous man," in whom is depicted the despair of the '80s, the logical conclusion of thirty years of Russian history combining in him a "great excitability, fatigue, feeling of guilt — all typically Russian traits."[6]

The peculiar dramatic structure of the play aroused unfavorable comment. Chekhov himself was not satisfied and with his usual humor called it a "dramatic abortion." Spurred, however, by his inclination to the theatre born long ago in his school years, he began the heavy task of

[5] Potapenko's recollections, in *Niva*, June-July, 1914.
[6] Chekhov to Suvorin, Dec. 30, 1888.

emodeling. In that revised form, *Ivanov,* at the instigation
of Suvorin, was given in St. Petersburg at the Alexandrine
Theatre (January 26, 1889) and *Novoe Vremya* greeted
the "extraordinary talent" of the young playwright (February 1, 1889).

This first serious dramatic work of Chekhov shows that
his observation and outlook on life were maturing, yet he
had a long way to go before he reached the perfection of
The Cherry Garden. Ivanov already has that "elfin strangeness," that peculiar slumber in which sink the heroes of
the Chekhov of later years. But the colors are not subdued
to a harmonious mellowness by the artful delicacy of his
touch. Though the aërial thinness of his bleak autumnal
day is yet lacking, one already feels the unfeigned sadness
of the nascent mood.

But he was still very young. He derived a particular joy
from the thought that the time of non-recognition was past.

"Let me tell you that in St. Petersburg, I am now a most
fashionable writer . . . The critics praise me to the skies
and insist that I am better than the other young writer,
Korolenko . . . My stories are read at the literary evenings. I am asked everywhere and new acquaintances crush
me, I have not one quiet day."[7]

The visits to St. Petersburg were like a honeymoon in
Chekhov's literary career. Suvorin, the poet Pleshcheyev,
and many gifted young people gathered together and spent
long evenings in discussions of life, art, and social problems. Chekhov was pleased; he regretted that he was unable
to live there forever. "In Petersburg I am in vogue like
Nana. At the same time that the publishers hardly
know the serious Korolenko, my rubbish is read by everybody. Even Senator G. reads it. Of course I am very much

[7] Chekhov to his uncle, M. G. Chekhov, Jan. 18, 1887.

flattered, but my literary sense is offended. I am ashamed of the public."[8]

In August, 1887, Suvorin published Chekhov's new miscellany, *V Sumerkakh* (In Twilight), containing sixteen of his best stories. This book was unanimously acclaimed and the young author was awarded by the Academy of Sciences half of the "Pushkin Prize, given for the best literary works." The joy of Anton Pavlovich is recorded in a letter to Suvorin (October 10, 1888): "I walk about as if I were in love. Father and Mother babble terrible nonsense and are unspeakably happy. Sister . . . ambitious and nervous, goes to her friends and spreads the news over the whole town. John Shcheglov talks about literary Jagos and the five hundred enemies I will acquire for the five hundred rubles I have received. Newspapermen of the second and third category should erect a monument in my honor or at least present me with a silver cigarette case. I cleared the way for them to the important magazines, to laurels, and to the hearts of decent people. For the present this is my only merit."

During the same period, so productive in his literary career, appeared two other books, *Nevinnia Riechi* (Innocent Talks) and *Razskasy* (Tales). The road to success was open. But when things look brightest, they are sometimes at their worst. Chekhov, admired and praised, felt uneasy: "I am too lucky. I have spent a wonderful summer . . . In September, I wrote a story for which I received three hundred rubles. And suddenly, like thunder from a clear sky this prize. I am too lucky . . . I begin to cast suspicious glances towards heaven. I shall hide myself quickly under the table and sit there tamely and quietly, without raising my voice."[9]

[8] Chekhov to Madame Kiseleva, Dec. 13, 1886.
[9] Chekhov to Suvorin, Oct. 10, 1888.

VII

East of the Sun, West of the Moon

THE years 1886-1889 were marked for Chekhov by great literary achievements. After the writing of the "Mass for the Dead," all his works showed a profound knowledge of human psychology beneath a truly artistic polish and grace. They presented a charming combination of smiles and sadness, of idealism and despair, of sensibility and intellectualism, which were a revelation to his amazed readers, who began to realize that those beautiful tales were created, not only by a real master with an extraordinary feeling for words, but also by the initiator of a new form of art — the short story.

To the casual observer Chekhov's joy in this recognition may appear boisterous. There was, however, under the seeming cheerfulness a deep concern over his failing health. After the pleasant visits to St. Petersburg other attacks of haemoptysis and constant fever held him in a state of nervous irritability. Tortured by nightmares, he wrote to Grigorovich (1887): "I see huge slippery stones, cold autumnal waters, bare coasts. I come upon broken cemetery gates and feel a ghastly chill which is impossible in reality." Yet this was the time of his real spiritual growth. The more intense his suffering became and the more life retreated, the more his work revealed its peculiar melancholy elusive-

ness. As if freed from the force of gravity, Chekhov began
to create his own literary form, intangible and musical, like
a chord in a minor key.

In the treasury of world literature, there are two works
of art, *The Mermaid* of Hans Christian Andersen and *La
Peau de Chagrin* of Honoré Balzac, which express the same
thought, that realization of desire brings sorrow and death.
Andersen in his charming fairy tale, which has the fresh-
ness and the melancholy of the North, tells us of a beautiful
mermaid who falls in love with a mortal. A powerful witch
transforms her tail into perfect little feet. The mermaid
joins her prince, but every time her foot touches the ground
she feels as if she were treading on sharp knives. Raphaël
de Valentin, in Balzac's novel, sees with terror that the
gratification of the least of his wishes produces a correspond-
ing shrinking in that parchment, the disappearance of
which means his own annihilation. So it was with Chekhov
who also walked on sharp knives towards recognition and
fame. He was always closely followed by his grim companion, the rapidly developing tuberculosis, and all his
desires were checked by the shadow of a premature end.
He had already begun to feel that *taedium vitae* which
made him consider human existence as an aimless joke.
Only the horror of black thoughts born of solitude, that
twin sister of death, urged him to receive his friends in
an uninterrupted procession: "I simply cannot live without guests," he wrote to Suvorin. "I am afraid to be
alone."[10] The title of his new book was chosen purposely;
In Twilight is an allegory — "life is dusk."[11] And to his
brother Mikhail, he spoke for the first time (March 10,
1887) the words which he was going to repeat until his
very end: "I am bored." Together with his heroes, "he

[10] Mikhail Chekhov, *Anton Chekhov*, pp. 49-50.
[11] Chekhov to his brother Alexander, May 25, 1887.

trailed his life out like an endless scarf."[12] Chekhov belonged to the lower middle class (*rasnochinets*) and felt unrooted since he had not yet found a solid social ground which would have relieved the tension he always experienced. "That which comes as a natural birthright to the writers of the nobility [like Turgenev and Tolstoy] the *rasnochintsy* buy with the price of their youth," he wrote in distress to Suvorin (January 7, 1889). He suffered from his own helplessness and exaggerated self-analysis. "I am fortune's obscure favorite who has jumped out of the bowels of the humorous little papers. . . . I am a *bourgeois-gentilhomme*, and such as these don't hold for very long, like a string that is stretched in the hurry."[13]

Work was the only remedy for his poverty and for the ever-growing sense of injustice and frustration. It was natural, then, that in his preoccupation with writing he should display, as he did, an aesthetic impassivity toward political and social questions that conveyed the impression of indifference to the welfare of his native land. He became a keen observer of everyday trivialities, in the light of which he now began to discern vanity and tragic misunderstanding as the ingredients of every human existence. Perplexed, like his gentle heroes, he thought that life was a strange dream oddly blended with reality: "We do not really live, it only seems that we do."[14] In the stillness of his feverish nights, in the weird land of the true and untrue, he conceived "Pari" (The Bet),[15] a beautiful story in which he presented the conclusion that everything on earth is "meaningless, transitory, shadowy, and delusive." Therefore, "one must live as Marcus Aurelius taught, to be ready at any

[12] *The Sea Gull*, Act II.
[13] Sobolev, in Koteliansky, *Anton Tchekhov, Literary and Theatrical Reminiscences*, p. 3.
[14] *The Three Sisters*, Act IV.
[15] Printed in *Novoe Vremya*, Jan. 1, 1889.

moment to meet death," the only thing on earth that has an eternal significance. Even beauty, which he "understood like lightning," conveyed to him a feeling of illusion and futility: "I felt beauty rather peculiarly. Masha awakened in me neither desire nor ecstasy nor delight, but a deep yet pleasant melancholy, dim and indefinable as a dream."[16] A painter in subdued tones, he purposely selected dim colors in order to impress his own mood on the reader, that particular mood which was later so skillfully expressed in his plays.

In "Ogni" (The Lights),[17] Engineer Ananiev reveals the crystallized pessimistic outlook of the author. "Then, in the '70s, it [pessimism] was fashionable in society and later passed from the public into literature, science, politics. I already knew that life is useless and meaningless, that everything is deceit and delusion. . . . One who knows that life is aimless and death inevitable is unwilling to cope with nature and is quite indifferent to the conception of sin." And he goes on to describe that utter loneliness, "when it seems that in the whole universe, sombre and amorphous, there is only one's self all alone . . . with thoughts of aimless life, of death, and of the darkness beyond."

"The Lights," although criticized for its "indifference" — which meant that no answers were given to the questions raised in the story — was quite significant. It aroused some dispute and caused Chekhov to send to Suvorin a letter (May 10, 1888) that is considered his literary credo: "You write that neither the discussion about pessimism nor the

[16] "Krasavitsy" (Beauties), *Novoe Vremya*, No. 4513, 1888.
[17] "Ogni" (The Lights), *Sieverny Viestnik*, No. 6. E. Werner, publisher of the magazine *Svierchok* (The Cricket), wrote to Chekhov, Aug. 8, 1888: "I read your 'Lights' and liked it very much, especially the conclusion, but nowadays and in this world not a jot of it could be understood."

story of Kissochka [the central feminine figure] unravels or solves problems such as God and pessimism. The writer has only to show how one may speak or think about God or pessimism, and in what circumstances. He is neither a judge of his characters nor of what they say, but an impartial witness."

Although aware of some qualities of his tale — "conciseness and a few new thoughts" — he was on the whole not satisfied. He wrote to his friend John Shcheglov (April 18, 1888), "I finished a boring story, meant to philosophize a little, but it turned out to be resin with vinegar." Chekhov was unnecessarily severe with himself. "The Lights" was most certainly real literature. It passed relatively unnoticed, however, because it was overshadowed by his long story, "The Steppe." In this the sadness of Russian horizons is symbolized by a tedious journey through the endless steppe, in the vast monotony of which motion is hardly more perceptible than rest. A strange boredom emanates from the wide expanse and is thrown into relief by the exquisite description of lightning and storm. The rain stops and the earth rests in the stillness of the blessed night. The author shows us "the stars which have looked down for many thousands of years, the deep mysterious sky indifferent to the short life of men." He also shows the men with masterful plasticity of representation: Father Christopher, the kind old priest, smelling of cypress; the strong healthy Dymov, whose excess of vitality is expressed in mischief; and little Iegoroushka, a boy of nine, who feels more than the others the utter sadness of the steppe.

"Dear Anton Pavlovich," wrote Pleshcheyev (February 8, 1888), "your tale is wonderfully poetic. I am in ecstasy. This is a great work and I predict for you a glorious future." Indeed, this story was outstanding, yet it failed in well-proportioned composition and was more like a number of short tales grouped together. "I am afraid I am not used to writing long stories," Chekhov explained to the poet Polonsky (January 18, 1888). Great was his relief when he realized that he had pleased the discriminating Pleshcheyev.

Chekhov's popularity grew with the publication of his stories in the *Sieverny Viestnik* (Messenger of the North). This outstanding periodical was edited during five years (1885-1890) by Anna Mikhailovna Ievreinova, the first Russian woman to receive her Ph.D. degree in Leipzig. Anton Pavlovich described her thus as "Ievreinova, an intelligent old maid — Doctor of Laws," and jokingly he called the *Sieverny Viestnik* a "literary old ladies' home."

He was, however, much pleased with this new connection and wrote to Grigorovich (October 9, 1888): "My short stories are printed in *Novoe Vremya*, but the longer ones in *Sieverny Viestnik*."

Everything on the surface looked so harmonious that the young man appeared satisfied and happy. He concealed his worries and even tried, in curiously didactic words, to encourage others: "Of course our existence is not easy, but you and I were not born into this vale of tears to experience the happiness of horse-guardsmen or actresses of the French theatre. We are lower middle class; we shall remain and die like them; such is fate."[18] It sounds almost cheerful and quite different from the Chekhov of the later years.

The writer Korolenko, who met him at this same period, wrote of the meeting: "I saw before me a young man looking even more youthful, a little over medium height, with a regular, clean-cut face which had not yet lost its characteristic boyish features. The simplicity of all his movements, manners, and speech was a predominant trait in his appearance, as in his writing. At that first meeting Chekhov

[18] Chekhov to Baranzevich, in Izmailov, p. 451.

made the impression on me of a profoundly cheerful man. It seemed that from his eyes flowed an inexhaustible stream of wit and spontaneous joy. Yet one could feel in him something deeper which was later to unfold and expand . . . The general impression he made on me was one of integrity and charm . . . and now when I remember the atmosphere of this closely united family in the center of which stood this charming and talented young man with such a gay outlook on life, it seems to me that it was the happiest, the last happy, streak of luck in the life of the whole family, a joyous idyll on the threshold of a drama."[19]

The summer of 1888 was, indeed, the last happy one in Chekhov's short life. A frequent guest in the house of Suvorin, he was joyfully received by the whole family, who adored him. July he spent at Suvorin's beautiful estate in Theodosia (Crimea). In August Chekhov with Suvorin's son took a journey through the Caucasus, the imposing majesty of which made a powerful impression on this son of the steppe. With but a few strokes he draws an amazing picture of his reaction: "It is a sublime poem . . . a beautiful fantastic tale written by Daemon in love with Thamar.[20] I am in Abkhasia [a province of Georgia on the Black Sea]. Nature is overwhelmingly beautiful. Everything is unexpected, fairy-like, absurd, and poetic . . . Eucalyptus trees, tea-roses, cypresses, cedars, palm-trees, donkeys, and mountains that are really mountains."

His ecstasy grew as he saw the famous Georgian Military Highway: "Imagine yourself at the height of 8,000 feet. Approach the edge of the precipice and look down. Far, far away you will see a narrow strip of land through

[19] Korolenko, I, 389-93.
[20] Chekhov to Suvorin, Aug. 12, 1888. "Daemon," a poem of Lermontov written under the influence of Byron. Daemon fell in love with Thamar, a beautiful Georgian Princess. D. S. Mirsky calls him the most unconvincing of demons. *History of Russian Literature*, p. 174.

which twists a white ribbon — this is the gray-haired, grumbling Aragva [river]. When you look down, your eyes meet clouds and woods, rocks and precipices. Now raise your eyes and look ahead of you. Mountains, mountains, and again mountains. Look upward, there is a deep blue sky. A fresh mountain breeze is blowing. Imagine two high walls and between them a long, long corridor. The ceiling is the sky, the floor, the Terek [river]. It unwinds like an ash-colored snake. The snake is furious and hisses. The horses fly like devils. From the top of the walls, trees bend curiously. One is dizzy. This is the Darial Pass, or, to use the language of Lermontov, 'The Narrows of Darial.' "[21]

In September Anton Pavlovich returned unwillingly to Moscow. He thought with nostalgia of his travels and freedom. To his friend, the writer Shcheglov, he complained (September 14, 1888) : "We are not living, we are losing our lives." For long hours, bent over his table, Chekhov wrote and wrote, remodeling and polishing his stories. The facility of his early years was gone: "Before I realized that my works were read and discussed I wrote undisturbed, as though I were eating pancakes [*bliny*], now I am writing in apprehension."[22]

His favorite brother, Nikolay, often played the piano for him. Inspired by the music of Chopin, Anton wrote "Imeniny" (The Party, 1888), a story justly considered one of his best; its treatment of feminine psychology combines medical thoroughness with impeccable literary form. But such was the trend of the times that a work of art was little appreciated, for the current tendency was to demand "the protesting element" in every serious literary work.

Chekhov, in surprisingly strong words, defended his in-

[21] Chekhov to Baranzevich, Aug. 12, 1888.
[22] Chekhov to Bilibin, Jan. 4, 1886.

dependence of popular standards: "I fear those who look for tendencies between the lines and try to see in me a liberal or a conservative. I am neither a liberal nor an evolutionist, neither a monk nor an indifferentist. I should like to be a free artist and that is all. My holy of holies is the human body, health, intelligence, talent, inspiration, love and the most complete freedom, freedom from despotism and lies."[23] Even the gentle Chekhov could fight in defense of his ideals. But after vehement outbursts he usually fell back into his customary meekness. After all, it was true that he was not interested in politics and social problems, which in bygone days tore the fiery soul of Dostoyevsky. Unable to feel strong impulses himself, he realized that he was not stirring human hearts and was not giving new impetus to life. "In our talents there is much phosphorus but no iron. Perhaps we are beautiful birds and sing well, but eagles we are not."[24]

The stagnation of the '80s made him lose courage; the time had passed when he was willing to have his works printed even on the window sill. Now he took his literary profession quite seriously. He complained to Suvorin (December 23, 1888) : "Why do I write? For the public? I don't see it. I believe in it less than in a ghost. To write for money? But I never have money and am quite reconciled to poverty. To write for praise would only irritate me. Literary Society, students, Ievreinova, Pleshcheyev laud my story, 'The Fit,' to the skies but the description of the first snow only Grigorovich noticed."

"Pripadok" (The Fit), quite a remarkable tale, was dedicated to the writer Garshin, who committed suicide in an attack of insanity. The charming Vsevolod Garshin, author of "Attalea Princeps," "Chetyre Dnia" (Four

[23] Chekhov to Pleshcheyev, Oct. 4, 1888.
[24] Chekhov to Shcheglov, Jan. 22, 1888.

Days), and "Krasny Tsvietok" (The Red Flower), was one of those "repentant noblemen" who considered it their duty to suffer with the people. This strange mania soon became morbid, his dissatisfaction with life grew, and feeling approaching madness, he threw himself down a flight of stairs (March 24, 1888). Delicate and sad, he had always attracted Chekhov, although they never met. There was a similarity between their talents, and "The Red Flower" (1883) gives us almost as deep an analysis of insanity as Chekhov's powerful "Ward Number 6," written nine years later. Garshin obviously bore the stigma of his degenerate age, that neurasthenia so skillfully presented in "The Fit." There we have the story of a young student who, confronted with the ugly side of life for the first time, is in a paroxysm of despair bordering on insanity, which Doctor Chekhov describes "according to the laws of psychiatry." A deep sadness permeates the tale — the evening, the dark sky, the wet snow — and fuses into a melancholy chord, sustained from the beginning to the end.

Chekhov, who always sought for new motifs and forms, had long ago broken with the old literary traditions. He avoided the narrow, stuffy atmosphere of the fossilized "circles" of his time. He believed "that new forms of literature produce new forms of life; that is why they are so revolting to the conservative human mind."[25]

Misunderstood and solitary, he wrote to Suvorin (May 4, 1889): "There is in my soul a sort of deadlock. I am not exactly disappointed or tired or melancholy — no, only everything has become less interesting." In "Skuchnaya Istoria" (The Dreary Story), published in 1889, he brings out with poignant clarity the complete isolation of the human soul, its gradual disillusionment with life. Not

[25] Chekhov, *Note-Books*, p. 10.

even science can console us. Contrary to "the established belief," it cannot give us answers to the important, primordial questions; we only know that we are "childlike, ignorant, superficial." All efforts are vain. The old professor, unhappy in his private life as well as in his work, already shows a strange *ataraxia*, that paralysis of the soul which was the reflection of Chekhov's own mood.

The type of the pedantic scientist, repeated later in Professor Serebriakov (in *Uncle Vanya*), provoked an outburst of indignation in university circles, but Chekhov, who was by this time quite used to harsh criticism, remarked philosophically: "I flatter myself with the hope that my rubbish will produce some noise and invective in the camp of the enemy. Without it nothing is possible in our century of the telegraph, Gorev's theatre, and telephones. Vituperation is kin to advertisement."[26] Indifferent to criticism as well as to praise, he published in 1889 another collection of stories significantly entitled *Khmurye Ludi* (Gloomy People).

This was the period of Anton Pavlovich's life when nature consoled him for all his sorrows. He loved to escape from Moscow, loved the summers, when the warm, sunny days created the illusion of well-being. "Under the influence of nature all the Petersburg 'tendencies' fade, even for those who have taken to heart the tricks of Mikhailovsky."[27] To him, serene or chaotic, nature seemed strangely alive in her manifestations. Lightning or clouds on the slopes of the Great Caucasus and pale flowers in the melancholy steppe were the reflections of the unknown God in whom Chekhov, the pantheist, believed after his own fashion: "Yes, Deacon, I believe in my way, not in

[26] Chekhov to Pleshcheyev, Sept. 14, 1889.
[27] Chekhov to Suvorin, June 28, 1888.

yours."[28] Yet his gentle soul, wearied by the grandiose effects of mountains and seas, sought rest in the green meadows and flowing brooks of the simple, unromantic landscapes of Russia.

For the summer of 1889 Chekhov rented a dilapidated estate in Luka (province of Khar'kov), which fourteen years later inspired the setting of his last play, *The Cherry Garden*. It was peaceful and soothing and dear to his heart, but, contrary to his expectations, it did not bring him the long-desired peace of body and mind. This was the beginning of long years of bad luck which struck Anton Pavlovich with implacable fury.

On June 17, his brother Nikolay died of tuberculosis. Anton Pavlovich never recovered from this greatest bereavement of his life. Although kind and friendly, he had few attachments, and the deepest of these was his affection for this favorite brother, the faithful companion of so many years. Together they had entered Vutsinas's temple of wisdom, together they had toiled in their father's grocery store, slunk to the theatre and improvised the next day. In Moscow, too, they had worked hand in hand. The cover of the *Tales of Melpomene* (1884) was designed by the gifted Nikolay, whom Anton believed to be the best man in the world. In profound affliction he wrote to Suvorin (July 2, 1889): "Poor Nikolay has died. I am stupid, extinguished." Overwhelmed by the catastrophe, his own health undermined by the same terrible illness, he felt that he was sinking into a chaotic darkness which froze his soul and robbed the outer world of its radiance.

It is interesting to note that at the same time in far-off France, Guy de Maupassant, with whom Chekhov was so

---

[28] Words of the zoologist von Koren in "The Duel" (1891). His conversation is Chekhov's reminiscence of his own long talks with the well-known zoologist, Professor V. A. Wagner.

often compared, passed through equally agonizing moments at the bedside of his brother, Hervé, who died on November 13, 1889, of paresis. The same disease caused Maupassant's death four years later (1893). Like Chekhov, he also died in July.

In the winter of 1889-1890 Chekhov's health took a decided turn for the worse. Frustrated in his affections and ambitions, he felt the need of a radical change. Only serious work could make him forget his sorrow and at the same time establish his reputation as a real observer of life. The serious work for him was a novel, which for some reason he could never write. His success as a writer of short stories he always accepted quite skeptically. And Chekhov, indifferent to the concern of his family and friends, decided to visit the Island of Saghalien, the Russian penal colony, to gather information about the life of the state criminals. The journey was conceived quite casually, according to his brother Mikhail, the jurist.

One day on reading the Penal Code, Anton Pavlovich said that convicts arouse interest only during their trial and are then forgotten and forsaken. He immediately began to plan his trip, but in such a manner that at first no one knew whether or not he was in earnest. He was not convinced that his trip would make any contribution either to literature or to science but believed that at least his new experiences would give him two or three days which he would remember all his life with happiness or sorrow. In vain his friends tried to persuade him that he should not risk his health. Obsessed by "Mania Sachalinosa," he wrote to Suvorin (March 9, 1889): "Saghalien is a place of unbearable sufferings. To such places we should go on a pilgrimage as Turks go to Mecca." And he carried out his plans with unexpected will power.

In the capacity of a newspaper correspondent, he set

out on April 20, 1890. Fortunately for us, Anton Pavlovich loved to write letters. At every stop on this long journey he sent his family and friends complete reports, which enable us to follow his impressions and experiences. Everything was new to him, the Yenisei, the vast forests of Siberia, the coachmen, the wild nature.

It was a long and difficult journey. The terrible cold at night, the heat of the day, the dust, the smoke of the forest fires certainly did not benefit his weak lungs, yet he stood his trip fairly well and laughed at all its discomforts.

After weeks, so ragged that "even tramps squinted at him," he finally arrived at Saghalien, where he was well received by the authorities. "From the very beginning," he wrote to Suvorin (September 11, 1890), "I have been in favorable circumstances and have seen everything and everyone. I got up every day at five o'clock and went to bed very late, thinking that much had yet to be done. I made a census of the population of Saghalien; in other words, there is not a convict or a settler who did not speak to me."

Children in the penal colony interested Chekhov greatly. He often talked with them, pitying these young souls for the dreadful conditions in which they had to live.

This intense work, which would have been strenuous even for a healthy man, soon exhausted Chekhov. Moreover, accustomed to a large family and to friends, he suffered terribly from solitude. At home, living among many people, he often felt the burden of human associations. Left alone, he experienced a dreadful sensation of anguish. He began once more to complain, as if he had been dragged to the Far East by sheer force. Saghalien annoyed him. For two months he had seen only convicts. He wrote to Suvorin (September 11, 1890): "I feel paralyzed when

I think that ten thousand versts separate me from the outer world. It seems to me that I will be home only in a hundred years! I am bored!"

Chekhov's life is the story of perpetual disillusionment. When he finally left the tragic island and sailed for Japan, China, and India, he was thrilled like a young boy who enjoys in advance the adventures which are bound to come in those exotic, mysterious lands. Indeed, the strange world which was revealed to him had the enchanting splendor of a fairy tale. Yet it did not disperse his melancholy. Crossing the ocean, Chekhov for the first time witnessed a burial at sea. Impressionable and nervous, brutally confronted with death, haunted by the horror of his own devastating illness which soon would reduce him to the state of that corpse thrown overboard, he became so depressed that he "nearly wept,"[29] forlorn amid the glorious but illusory beauty. He longed for companionship most of all. Nevertheless, he declined casual acquaintances. When a young painter wanted to join him for the remainder of the trip Chekhov begged the friend who introduced them: "Be my benefactor, tell N. that I am a drunkard, a swindler, a nihilist, a ruffian, that no one should ever go with me, that travel in my society would be a failure. Tell him not to waste time with me."[30]

In that complex nature, full of inhibitions and fears, feelings were more or less contradictory. Peace became unobtainable for a mind tortured by sorrow and illness. Weakness of body paralyzed his will and kept him in strange dim realms of twilight. It was that same odd numbness, that curse of his generation, which in a more pronounced form led the charming Vsevolod Garshin to suicide and caused the brilliant Vladimir Soloviev to live

[29] Chekhov to Suvorin, Dec. 9, 1890.
[30] Izmailov, p. 318.

in a mystic world of his own, immersed in the doctrine of Sophia, the Divine Wisdom.

On December 9, 1890, Chekhov arrived in Moscow and brought with him, besides the memory of his personal experiences, a vast amount of material about the penal colony, "sufficient for three dissertations." Soon there appeared in *Russian Thought* a series of articles under the title "The Island of Saghalien" (1891).[31] After their publication some reforms were brought about on the terrible island. Thirty years before, Dostoyevsky had profoundly stirred Russian society with his famous *Memoirs of the House of the Dead*. Chekhov now provided another instance of the humanitarian influence of literature.

Six months of travel had exhausted Anton Pavlovich. He looked tired and gloomy. His family lived in a small and crowded apartment which seemed unbearable after wide spaces and freedom. Moscow, an alluring mirage seen from afar, proved in reality to be uninteresting and dull. Suddenly the impressions made upon him by the colorful Orient, now that they were swept into the past, were magnified in his imagination. Like Sindbad the Sailor, he yearned for new adventures: "I shall work all winter uninterruptedly in order to go to Chicago in the spring and from there across America to Japan and India."[32]

At times he was anxious to visit his faithful Suvorin in St. Petersburg. Then again he wrote to his friends: "Why are we not in Paris?"[33] From now on until his death he would complain about his boredom. His letters illustrate his prevailing melancholy mood. To Suvorin, October 18,

[31] Upon returning he printed "Ubiistvo" (Murder), "V Ssylke" (In Banishment) and "Gusev." In this last story he describes a consumptive soldier, on his way home from the Far East, who dies in mid-ocean.

[32] Chekhov to Suvorin, Oct. 18, 1892.

[33] Chekhov to Chervinsky, Oct. 25, 1891.

1892, he wrote: "As a true physician, I am fully, almost cynically, convinced that from this life one can expect only the worst." To Suvorin again in 1893: "All my university colleagues are already civilian counselors. Only I am not worth a fig." And again, August 18, 1893: "That indolent state of mind, depriving me of will, lasts sometimes whole months." Trigorin, a character in *The Sea Gull*, says: "I have no will of my own. I never have had, I am too indolent, too submissive, too phlegmatic." To Suvorin, Chekhov wrote in 1895: "I am bored, I don't know what to do with my own person." And he makes Trigorin say again: "I cannot escape from myself." To Suvorin, July 11, 1897: "Too bad life drags so monotonously and inertly." And to Gorky, February 15, 1900: "I am bored." When in June, 1904, a month before his death, he went to a health resort in the Schwarzwald, Chekhov, although accepting his inevitable fate, remained true to his habit of complaining and wrote: "What a terrible bore is this German health resort, Badenweiler."[34]

The work on Saghalien, "this beloved brain-child," greatly consoled him. He felt satisfaction in having produced a serious work. After its publication he wrote to Suvorin (January 2, 1894): "I am glad that these stiff prison overalls hang in my literary wardrobe."

At that period Chekhov wrote frequently to his old friend. His recent visit to St. Petersburg fully convinced him that Suvorin was the only person who had for him a sincere affection. All his other contemporaries and acquaintances met him with enmity or jealousy. He wrote to his sister (January, 1891): "I am surrounded by an atmosphere of evil and indefinite feelings. I am invited to dinners, flooded with banal compliments and at the same time know that they are ready to swallow me. They

[34] Chekhov to Professor Rossolimo, in Izmailov, p. 522.

are not people, but mud." He returned to Moscow lacking that exaltation of spirits usually noticeable after his visits to St. Petersburg.

The long journey to the Far East exhausted also the finances of Anton Pavlovich, who, despite his popularity, was poor. The plate with the name "Dr. Chekhov" had long since disappeared from his door with no regret on his part. Writing was now his only means of subsistence. Impractical, overburdened with responsibilities, he was never able to balance his budget so as to live in comfort and peace. To Suvorin again he confided his troubles (July 24, 1891) : "To make a fortune, to escape the abyss of petty worries and fears, I have only one choice, an immoral one, to marry into wealth or to say that *Anna Karenina* is my novel."

Chekhov loved to stroll in the winding streets of Moscow. Dissatisfied with reality, he dreamed again of new wanderings in search of happiness in some distant land, east of the sun, west of the moon. He was afflicted with that confusion of soul, that eternal yearning for something vague and unattainable, that desire to take a staff in hand and go — a trait deeply rooted in the national character of Russians, from aristocrat to beggar.[35]

Suvorin, always affectionate and thoughtful, watched his friend with concern. In all the years of their friendship he never failed in his role of the kind *Fée Mélusine*,[36] ready to appear whenever Chekhov needed him. He sug-

---

[35] Everybody knows of the famous "escape" of Count Leo Tolstoy, his wanderings, and finally his death at Astapovo (Nov. 7, 1910). According to a wide-spread legend, the Emperor Alexander I did not die Nov. 19, 1825, but left everything and went to Siberia as a wanderer under the name of Fedor Kusmich. As for poor people, Russia always had a swarm of wanderers, striving mostly for the Holy Land or Mount Athos. They were considered as saints and were very well treated by the population.

[36] Mélusine, a fairy, popular in the novels of chivalry, protectress of the house of Lusignan.

gested a trip; Anton Pavlovich accepted as a means of interrupting his bothersome, prosaic life.

On March 19, 1891 the two friends left St. Petersburg for Southern Europe. Their goal was Italy, which Suvorin wanted to show to Chekhov. They arrived on a beautiful spring day. "The blue-eyed Venice" enchanted Anton Pavlovich. He wrote to his brother Ivan (March 24, 1891): "All here is loveliness and glitter and happiness of life." He wandered with delight through the streets as in Moscow, and sat for hours in St. Mark's Cathedral, which reminded him of the Byzantine churches of his country. He loved to ride in gondolas through the canals, in the sparkling Italian sun. He admired the graceful bridges, the picturesque squares. He wished to stay there forever.

Yet with the first rain all magic vanished. There was no more room for happy emotions in this wounded soul. Quickly fatigued, he was not able to keep pace with the healthy Suvorin. Constant visits to art galleries and to churches were beyond his strength. Exhaustion made him say one day that he would like to rest in the meadows near Moscow, a remark which seemed to prove that his reputation for indifference to foreign countries was well founded. Suvorin was surprised: "He was not interested in art, statues, pictures, cathedrals. . . . Venice impressed him with its originality, its life and serenades, but not with the Palace of the Doges. He was interested in graveyards and circuses with clowns — thus illustrating the two sides of his talent, the comic and the tragic, sorrow and humor, tears and laughter over his fellowmen and himself."[37]

Indeed, Chekhov had a strange passion for graveyards and visited them wherever he was: "I shall be in Taganrog

[37] Suvorin, "Malen'kie Pis'ma" (Short Letters), *Novoe Vremya,* No. 10179, July 4, 1904.

one, two, three days, shall take a swim, visit the local cemetery, and then return."[38] Many an anecdote has been recorded of his morbid inclination. Once he came to the city of Perm', which he hardly knew, and went immediately to the cemetery. His admirers, who watched attentively every step of their celebrated guest, imagined an old romance. They tried to discover who had been the lady so fortunate as to win his heart. Later they learned that wherever he was he went for a solitary walk in the cemetery.[39] He loved to wander among the tombs "because in every poplar tree one feels mystery, and the gravestones and the faded flowers, together with the autumnal fragrance of leaves, breathe pardon, sadness, and peace."[40]

The well-known Russian writer, Dimitrii Merezhkovsky, who met Chekhov in Venice, was startled by his indifference. "I spoke enthusiastically about Italy. He was walking beside me, tall, slightly bent, as usual smiling quietly. He also was in Italy for the first time; Venice was for him, as for me, the first Italian city. However, no exultation was noticeable in him. It even offended me. He was occupied by trifles unexpected and, as it seemed to me then, even uninteresting: a guide with a very bald head, the voice of the girl selling violets on St. Mark's Square, the uninterrupted bells at the Italian stations."[41]

Chekhov, with his literary culture predominant, was indifferent to other forms of art. Under the restrictive influence of his early environment he did not develop the receptiveness of the upper classes. The philosophical

[38] Chekhov to Suvorin, July 11, 1894.
[39] Professor Batushkov, in Pokrovsky, *Kriticheskaya Antologia* (Critical Anthology).
[40] Chekhov's own words in his story "Ionych," in the Marks edition of Chekhov's works, XII, 49.
[41] Feider, p. 184.

meditations of the '40s stressed their inherent love for abstract questions, the quest for the "higher synthesis," which they found only in beauty. Brought up in the monotony of their icy plains, in the poverty of their unromantic scenery, they readily left Russia for the blue splendor of the Mediterranean and in the Parthenon or on the Palatine they dreamt of the past grandeur of ancient civilizations.

Yet, once they were established in Italy or Greece, away from the daily routine of home, they had moments of bitter nostalgia when they felt for their distant land love and longing, which in the Russian soul is always the most lasting emotion.

Gogol, who lived for twelve years in Rome, expressed this feeling exquisitely: "Russia, I see thee from my wondrously beautiful, distant abode, I see thee. . . . There is nothing in thee to fascinate, to allure the eye. . . . But what impenetrable, mysterious force draws one to thee? . . . Why does thy melancholy song, floating all over thy width and length from sea to sea, resound unceasingly in the ear? . . . Is it not there, not in thee that boundless thought should be born since thou art boundless thyself? . . . What a marvelous, radiant expanse, unknown to the earth! Russia . . ."[42] Artistic, unsettled, inconstant were the restless children of that feminine land, for "Russia herself, as has been observed, is a woman nation."[43]

Such was not the case with Chekhov, the *rasnochinets*, whose restlessness was more of a nervous than of an artistic nature. Attached to his family, who idolized him, he longed for his home, for Russian dishes. He felt that he was stripped of artistic appreciation, and though he was usually so gentle, he defended himself in an angry outburst:

[42] Gogol, *Mertvia Dushy* (Dead Souls), p. 231.
[43] Graham, *Undiscovered Russia*, p. 327.

"What had I to do? Shout from exaltation? Break windows? Embrace Frenchmen?"[44] And he returned home as truly Russian as he had ever been. His writings, deeply rooted in his native soil, always had for their background Mother Russia and did not reflect the impressions of the West. Only in "Ariadna" (1893) and in "The Tale of the Unknown Man" (1893) do we find reminiscences of Italy. Yet a new, important trait was born in him in all his traveling. Chekhov always feared annihilation. His mind, tortured by insoluble questions of life and death, unable to penetrate their mystery, sought consolation in timid attempts to find some faith. This is already noticeable in "The Duel" (1891) and is even more pronounced in "The Tale of the Unknown Man," which depicts a man who, also consumptive and sad, looked at the house of Desdemona in Venice, "the melancholy little house, light as lace," and thought: "Ah, if to all this peaceful rest and contentment there could be added a tiny bit of some faith."[45] In the *Note-Books* of Anton Pavlovich we find another interesting thought: "Faith is a spiritual faculty. Animals do not have it. Savages and uncivilized people have merely fear and doubt. Only highly developed natures have faith." It seemed as though the thirty-two-year-old Chekhov were looking for some definite anchorage which would offer him physical and mental peace.

[44] Chekhov to Suvorin, May 27, 1891.
[45] Anton Chekhov, "Razskaz Neizvestnago Cheloveka" (The Tale of the Unknown Man), in the Marks edition of Chekhov's works, IX, 77.

VIII

The "Duchy" of Melikhovo

LONGING for the peace and coziness of a real home led Chekhov to buy Melikhovo, a dilapidated country house only a short distance from Moscow. "This property was nothing more than an uncomfortable cottage, large vacant lots, and trees." But the first impression on Anton Pavlovich was favorable. He made the purchase in the winter of 1892 and moved in at once, delighted to leave the noise of the city behind him. Melikhovo soon improved visibly under the efforts of the family, whom Chekhov was happy to reunite. It seemed very much like the old days in Taganrog, except that the grumbling father had quieted down considerably and Anton had become the uncontested master of the house. "In the largest room with windows on all sides, he had his study. Very early in the morning, sometimes at four o'clock, he was up. After his coffee he went to the garden where he loved to plant trees and rosebushes. Lunch over, he shut himself into his bedroom and wrote. The hours from tea to dinner were consecrated to rest and walks. At ten o'clock in the evening everyone went to bed, lights were extinguished, and the house became silent. One could hear only singing in a low voice and monotonous reading.

This was Pavel Iegorovich, who was saying vespers in his room."[46]

"I am living here as in Australia, somewhere at the edge of the world," Chekhov wrote to Suvorin (March 17, 1892). "My frame of mind is good." Accompanied by his fat little dogs that answered to the amusing names "Bromide" and "Quinine," he loved to walk through his "duchy," surprised at being a landowner. "I stand under the tree and eat cherries. It seems so strange that nobody chases me away. As a boy, my ears were daily boxed for eating them."[47]

Those casual words recall the hardships of his childhood when thrashings were an inescapable part of his life. One can surmise that for Chekhov's "inferiority complex" there was a profound psychological reason, something more than his pathological condition and the general gloom of his epoch. It is significant that in his literary work, which reflects his real ego, his characters are, like himself, lost in this puzzling world, deprived of will, in quest of happiness, for the attainment of which they have no power to struggle. For the Russian reader the charm of his unheroic heroes lay in their very weakness. The profound compassion aroused by their invariable surrender could be explained by a national trait, predominant since the dawn of Russian history, the inclination less to love than to pity. That Russian pity, often discussed at the time of Gogol and Dostoyevsky, can be found in the earliest monuments of national literature. In the famous epic of the twelfth century, *The Word of the Regiment of Igor,* the most sublime passage is the lament of Yaroslavna, who, while addressing "the bright,

[46] Mikhail Chekhov, *Anton Chekhov,* pp. 90-93.
[47] Chekhov to Suvorin, July 3, 1892.

thrice-bright sun," mourns for her beloved husband, Prince Igor, fallen into the hands of the enemy.

A romantic attachment seems to be unknown to Russians; it belongs rather to the Germano-Roman civilization together with the cult of the Madonna and chivalry. Chekhov, that melancholy bard of his crepuscular land, responded more than his predecessors to this fundamental need of the Russian soul — pity — with which his own tenderness was in complete accord. This tenderness combined with his own misfortunes made Chekhov not only depict the misfit but also glorify failure with an unsurpassed poignancy, which appealed to Russians, who were profoundly unadapted to life.

"The position of Melikhovo on the main road and the news that the writer Chekhov had established himself there inevitably brought new acquaintances."[48] He received visits from the neighboring medical men and members of the district council. His kindness made him very popular among the peasants, to whom he never refused either professional or financial help. Patients came to him from twenty and twenty-five versts away. Early in the morning many people were waiting for medical care in front of his house. Now and then Chekhov complained: "Friends, what a bore! If I am a physician, I need not only patients but hospitals. If I am a writer, I have to live among people."[49] During the cholera epidemics (1892), he offered his services as a district physician without remuneration, although he resented the burden of this busy life: "My soul is tired. What a bore! Never to belong to myself, but to have to think about diarrhea, to be startled every night by the barking of the dog and knocks at the gate (is it not for me that they come?), to

[48] Mikhail Chekhov, *Anton Chekhov*, pp. 98-100.
[49] Chekhov to Suvorin, Oct. 19, 1891.

drive terrible horses through unknown roads . . . this, my dear sir, is a mess which does not do me any good."[50]

At the same time the realization that he had to write and keep on writing began to poison his existence. Despite general recognition, the literary path of Chekhov was far from rose-strewn. With his usual tact, he knew how to shun the severity of the censorship, but he could not escape the animosity of the rancorous Mikhailovsky, who never forgot how firmly and resolutely Anton Pavlovich had refused his unasked advice.

Early in the spring of 1892, Chekhov published a story "based on philosophical speculation, but devoid of the element of love," as he described it to Suvorin (March, 1892). This was "Ward No. 6," a masterpiece, in which, with great penetration and power, he analyzed the tortured mind of a psychiatrist confined in his own insane asylum. Realistic to the smallest detail, he revealed skillfully the emotional tenseness of Doctor Ragin, who, whether insane or not — we do not know — dies from despair among his former patients.

The effect created by the artistic impassivity and the sobriety of narration was tremendous, yet Mikhailovsky started once more his campaign against Chekhov. "In selecting his subjects, he is never guided by *principles*; that is the way of Mr. Chekhov." While accusing him of "indifference and apathy," the critic mourned that Russian literature had lost in Chekhov a great writer. This dislike grew continually, and when Anton Pavlovich published "The Peasants," a great sensation of 1897, Mikhailovsky met it with more harsh criticism. But Chekhov remained unmoved. Already in 1890 he wrote with his usual keenness to his friend Shcheglov (March 22) : "The criticism is either firmly silent or gets off cheaply with idle

[50] Chekhov to Suvorin, Aug. 16, 1892.

trashy chatter. If it [the criticism] impresses you, it is because it is an empty barrel which makes much noise."

Chekhov did not yield in the pursuit of what was for him artistic truth, yet, distressed by the eternal persecution of his literary enemies, he turned his eyes towards the "Great Old Man," Count Leo Tolstoy, and sought consolation in his friendship and philosophy. Whether or not he was influenced by Tolstoy's teaching it is difficult to say, since we have Chekhov's own contradictory statements. He wrote to Suvorin on August 30, 1891: "I should like to have rugs, a fire place, bronzes and intelligent conversation. Alas, I shall never be a Tolstoyist. In women, above all, I love beauty, and in the history of mankind the culture expressed in rugs, in carriages on springs, and in clear thoughts." And to Suvorin again on March 27, 1894: "Tolstoy's philosophy influenced me very deeply for six or seven years, and impressed me, not by the basic principles, which were known to me before, but by Tolstoy's manner of expression — a rationalism and probably a hypnotism of some kind. Now something in me rebels against it. Reason and justice tell me that in electricity and steam there is more love for mankind than in chastity and abstinence from meat. . . . War is an evil and litigation is an evil, but it does not follow that I have to wear bast-shoes and sleep in filth with the workman and his wife. It is no more a matter of 'pro or con'; the point is that Tolstoy has already faded, he is no longer in my soul."

On January 28, 1900 he wrote again to Suvorin: "His illness frightens and unnerves me. I fear the death of Tolstoy. If he should die, there would be a great emptiness in my life. First of all, I never loved anyone as I love him; I am an unbeliever, but of all faiths his is the nearest and the most congenial to me. . . . When there is a Tolstoy, it is pleasant and agreeable to be a writer. . . .

Moreover, Tolstoy stands firm, his authority is tremendous, and as long as he lives, bad taste in literature, triviality, impertinence, bitterness will be relegated to the shadows. . . . Only his great moral authority is able to keep on a certain height the so-called literary tendencies and currents. There would be great confusion without him."

This last statement, written four years before Chekhov's death, expresses his fully mature thought. It seems as though he accepted Tolstoy rather as a literary authority than as a philosophical teacher. Yet during seven years, 1889-1896, the writing of Anton Pavlovich shows a strong influence of Tolstoy's tenets. In "The Dreary Story" (1889), we see the old professor dissatisfied with science and the life he has led; he dies alone, misunderstood and vain. In "The Princess" (1889), we have the picture of a stupid, frivolous woman, who embodies the selfishness of high society. In the beautiful tale, "My Life" (1896), the hero, Polosnev, glorifies physical labor; he tries to solve his problems by abandoning artificial civilization and merging with the working classes.

But in a final analysis Tolstoy's philosophy never relieved Chekhov's pessimism. Chekhov, with his sober mind, realized that the splitting of the human entity by separating the spiritual ego from the physical being had never been justified by nature and, therefore, could not be true. The conception of freedom as external and internal, the non-resistance to evil, the denial of pain, seemed like a profanation to Chekhov, who, as a physician, was conscious of the dependence of individuals upon environment. Doctor Ragin, in conversation with the insane Ivan Dimitrievich, claimed first that there was no difference between life outside and life in Ward No. 6, as long as "one feels free," yet when he himself was confined in the asylum, he saw the "difference" and died from despair.

In one of his best stories, "The Gooseberries" (1898),[51] when Anton Pavlovich, freed from all influences, found his own way, he wrote that to leave the cities for the country, to hide in one's own land (perhaps he meant Tolstoy himself) was no life, but selfishness and laziness. "Man needs not only three yards of earth [for his grave], but the whole world in which he can express all the peculiarities and capacities of his unbounded spirit."

Chekhov's admiration for Tolstoy, however, was sincere and lasting. On his part, Tolstoy, though criticizing Chekhov's "feminine" plays, utterly incomprehensible to his virile genius, fully recognized the supreme mastery of Chekhov's charming tales. "No one of the Russian writers was read so often and with so much pleasure at the house of Tolstoy as Chekhov," Sergeyenko informs us. One day, upon reading "The Darling," Tolstoy said: "This is a real pearl, truly an excellent story."[52]

In the years 1894-1896 Chekhov saw Tolstoy frequently, and twice visited him on his estate, Yasnaya Poliana. They even planned to go together to America.[53] This voyage, however, never took place.

Chekhov, though not forgetting his wanderlust, seemed to be well established in Melikhovo. Guests were almost permanent in his attractive country house.

Obliged to entertain his many visitors, he often worked and meditated at night. Life, as ever, fascinated him. Against its background of iniquity and cruelty, he saw the touching and the noble in the human soul, and these sound through his stories like the echo of a beautiful

[51] "Kryzhovnik."

[52] Sergeyenko's recollections, in *Niva*, Oct., 1904.

[53] Chekhov wrote to Ilia Repin, a well-known Russian painter, Jan. 22, 1896: "Tolstoy came to see me and we decided to go to America."

song. Sometimes he complained that there was not enough stimulation around him: "Always the same thing! I should love to write about devils, about terrible, volcanic women and sorcerers, but alas! seemingly only tales from the lives of Ivan Gavrilovichs and their spouses are in demand."[54]

The sobriety of his condensed literary form made him look for the very essence of life, stripped of any unnecessary burden of words. The avoidance of spectacular and startling effects was especially suitable for his unheroic heroes, who call to mind the characters of Samuel Butler. Chekhov's search for simplification, for the mere scheme of human existence, is illustrated by Madame Shchepkina-Kupernik, known in Russian letters for her skillful translation of Edmond Rostand's *La Princesse lointaine*. "One day," Madame Kupernik tells us, "after a rain we went towards the house, and Chekhov, holding a wet umbrella, said: 'Somebody ought to write a vaudeville sketch. Two people wait in an empty barn for the rain to pass. They joke, they laugh, they dry their umbrellas, make love to each other. Then the rain stops, there is sunshine, and suddenly he dies from heart failure.' 'Good heavens!' I exclaimed in surprise. 'What kind of vaudeville would that be?' 'Well,' he answered, 'such is life, is it not? We joke and laugh and then — bang! All is over.' "[55]

On the same occasion Chekhov showed Madame Kupernik his *Note-Books* — a privilege extended only to close friends. These *Note-Books*, carefully kept 1891-1904, seem to have been his secret "literary store-room" where he gathered together random impressions and thoughts:

Why did Hamlet trouble about ghosts after death, when life itself is haunted by ghosts so much more terrible?

[54] Chekhov to Helena Mikhailovna Sh., Dec. 24, 1894.
[55] Feider, p. 246.

[110]

Perhaps the universe is suspended on the tooth of some monster.

Russia is nobody's country.

Death is terrible, but still more terrible is the feeling that one may live forever and never die.

Senile pomposity, senile vindictiveness — what a number of despicable old people I have known!

Russia is an enormous plain across which wander mischievous men.

Now and then we find glimpses of his usual humor:

A man of eighty says to a man of sixty: "You ought to be ashamed, young man."

"Love? In love? Never! I am a Government clerk."

Among the frequent guests at Melikhovo one person especially interested Chekhov. This was Lika Misinova, a friend of his sister Masha. She usually came with the writer Potapenko, to the great delight of the whole family. After dinner the two visitors would sometimes sing Braha's popular "Wallachian Legend," in which a dying girl hears mysterious calls and sees angels but cannot make her mother believe her. Beautiful nights, the fragrance of flowers, and the presence of Lika animated Anton Pavlovich, who, after long walks, loved to sit on the porch and philosophize.

"One evening," his brother Mikhail relates, "when the sun like a red and tremendous ball neared the horizon, the question was brought up why, when it goes down, it becomes red and seems larger than during the day. After a long debate, it was decided that at such moments, when it is below the horizon, the air, like a prism, reflects its rays; the sun, losing its natural coloring, appears much larger than in the daytime. Thereafter we spoke about mirages and reflections of rays in the air, and, as a result, the question rose as to whether the mirage itself could be

reflected in the air and produce another mirage. It seemed
as though it could. And this second mirage can give rise
to the third and then the fourth and so on eternally
Therefore, it is possible that in the universe there are
mirages reflecting localities and even people and animals
of a thousand years ago. . . . Of course, this was young
people's chatter, but the solving of those questions inter
ested everybody in Melikhovo at that time. One afternoon
Anton Pavlovich came out of his room and began to
walk up and down, strangely rubbing his eyes and fore
head. . . . 'A while ago I had a terrible dream. I saw a
black monk.' The impression of this dream was so strong
that he could not compose himself for a long time. Those
who have read 'The Black Monk' will, I think, understand
its origin and structure and will recognize in it the 'Wal
lachian Legend' and the talks about mirages."[56]

Chekhov combined his dream with reality in describing
Kovrin, an overworked scholar who, in his hallucinations
sees the "Black Monk" — a strange mirage reflected in
the air — and is ready to follow him to the mysterious
distant worlds.

Izmailov, Chekhov's biographer, has pointed out as a
significant fact that Kovrin and Doctor Ragin, the "other
noble madman" of "Ward No. 6," are the only characters
among Chekhov's heroes who talk about eternity and the
immortality of the soul.

"No matter what glorious dawn should lighten your
life," says Doctor Ragin to his patient, Ivan Dimitrievich
"nevertheless, at the end you will be placed in a casket
and thrown into a grave."

"And immortality?"

"Oh, nonsense!"

"You do not believe, but I do. In Dostoyevsky or Vol

[56] Mikhail Chekhov, *Anton Chekhov*, pp. 106-10.

ire some one said that if there were no God he would
e invented by man, and I believe deeply that if there
ere no immortality the great human mind, sooner or
iter, would invent it."

And the Black Monk consoles the visionary Kovrin,
ying of consumption, by saying: "There is an eternal
fe."

"What is the goal of eternal life?" asks Kovrin.

"Joy! True joy is knowledge, and eternal life will pre-
:nt endless and infinite sources of knowledge."

Chekhov rarely discussed immortality and faith, but
hen he did one could feel profound conflicts between
is aspiration for greater realities and his materialistic
lucation. The study of medicine made him confront life
ith a skeptical eye. Still we do not know what were his
mermost thoughts, concealed from everyone with his
sual reticence. In a curious letter to Suvorin (January
5, 1894), he explained: "If the author describes insanity,
does not mean that he himself is insane. I wrote 'The
lack Monk' without despondency. I simply had the de-
re to depict a case of megalomania. As for a monk slid-
ig through the fields, I dreamt about him and, upon
wakening, related it to Misha [Mikhail Chekhov]. There-
ire, please tell Anna Ivanovna [Madame Suvorina] that
oor Anton Pavlovich, thank heavens, is not yet mad, but
its too much at supper and sees monks in his dreams."

Since the letters of Suvorin have not been found, we
o not know what remark on his part provoked this an-
ver. It may be that the secretive Chekhov, in order to
ide his ideas of life and death, characterized them inten-
onally as the hallucinations of a madman. A timid na-
ire, like Chekhov's, is reluctant to permit anyone to lift
ie curtain that hides its ego, the depths of which we

shall never know. The faith of such, like their love, r
mains a profound secret.

Chekhov very seldom spoke about love. One gener
statement he made would, however, permit one to co
clude that this emotion had not deeply stirred his hear
"Love!" he wrote, "Either it is a remnant of somethin
degenerating, something which has once been immens
or it is a particle of what in the future will develop int
something immense; but in the present it is unsatisfyin
it gives much less than one expects."[57]

What his own attachment to Lika was, no one can sa
Lika is the only woman known to have played an impo
tant role in his life until his late marriage. Yet she di
not awaken any strong feeling in the weary soul o
Chekhov, who acted as though he were surrounded b
the cool breeze of the steppe. It seems likely that Lik
was merely a friend, with whom he took pleasure in tall
ing in the gay and flirtatious manner men often assume i
a relationship with pretty women whom they would nev
admit to their inner realm. Moreover, it does not appe
that he greatly admired women in general. "What a lot
idiots there are among ladies! People have got so used
it that they no longer notice it."[58] And he used to sa
"If you are afraid of loneliness, do not marry."

Love had certainly not been a deep source of emotio
for the man whose motto was "I do not want a thing
Chekhov, in fact, was rapidly growing old; his detac
ment or indifference became more obvious with eve
year. Only his restlessness remained always the same: "
I had had money, I would have gone to South Ameri
. . . one needs an aim in life, in travel there is an aim."

In his soul, there remained an ever-present pain, an

[57] Chekhov, *Note-Books*, p. 36.   [58] *Ibid.*, p. 87.
[59] Chekhov to Lika Misinova, Aug. 15, 1893.

he long evenings in Melikhovo, with drawn curtains and oft lamplight, had already ceased to create the pleasant ensation of security. He was often surrounded by people ae hardly knew. Curious students, neighbors, and medical nen considered it their duty to pay him a visit and even ,o stay overnight. Sometimes they were so numerous that ill the rooms in the house were occupied. Chekhov, despite the habitual grace of his hospitality, felt exhausted: 'Guests, guests, guests! Of course, it is pleasant to be hospitable, but there is a limit to everything. I left Moscow o escape guests."[60]

In this heterogeneous crowd he had the odd feeling of an utter loneliness of soul, which he so dreaded and which, ike an evil shadow, haunted him all his life. His favórite brother, Nikolay, who could have comforted him, had rested for many years in a distant cemetery under poplars ind weeping willows. Suvorin, healthy and strong, surrounded by family and friends, led an active life in St. Petersburg. And Chekhov, forlorn and ill, oppressed with financial worries, stood in the midst of his darkest years when literature alone remained his faithful companion.

[60] Chekhov to Suvorin, Dec. 8, 1893.

IX

Autumnal Chant

Les sanglots longs
Des violons
De l'automne
Blessent mon cœur
D'une langueur
Monotone.

Tout suffocant
Et blême, quand
Sonne l'heure,
Je me souviens
Des jours anciens
Et je pleure.

Et je m'en vais
Au vent mauvais
Qui m'emporte
Deçà, delà,
Pareil à la
Feuille morte.

—— PAUL VERLAINE

THOSE who have read "The Steppe" will readily agree
that Chekhov loved nature, which, as it seemed to him,
was able to heal all the sorrows and ills of the earth.
Therefore it is not surprising that when the need of peace
for work and rest became urgent, his first thought was to
seek refuge in a remote part of his large garden. Here he
built a little house in the spring of 1895. The view of the

ake and the old trees from his new study was magnificent, especially at sunset and in the moonlight. In that tiny dwelling, away from the noise of tiresome callers, he was to create *Chaïka* (The Sea Gull), his first drama of mood.

On May 5, 1895, Chekhov notified Suvorin that he would write a comedy for his "Little Theatre," which had offered Hauptmann's *Hannele*[61] as its first production. "I shall write something strange," he promised, and started to work at once. Yet he felt ill at ease. Although passionately interested in the theatre, he could not forget that *Ivanov* had met with disapproval in Moscow and that its dubious success in St. Petersburg had been the result of Suvorin's flattering articles.

On the other hand, Anton Pavlovich's vaudeville act, "The Bear" (1888), was, despite its "absurdity," very popular on every stage.[62] In 1888 Chekhov had attempted once more to write a play, *The Wood Spirit*, which proved, like *Ivanov*, a failure. It was a peculiar comedy. "I am surprised," Chekhov said, "that such strange things come from my pen." As usual, he made fun of himself because the "two first acts were spent in conversation and food," and he explained: "Let's just be as complex and as simple as life is. People dine and at the same time their happiness is made or their lives are broken."[63] It is interesting to note that Maeterlinck, the father of the lyrical-static drama, expressed himself almost in the same words: "It is in a small room, round the table, close to the fire, that the joys and sorrows of mankind are decided. We suffer, or make others suffer, we love, we die, there in our corner."[64]

[61] Gerhart Hauptmann, *Hanneles Himmelfahrt* (1892).

[62] Chekhov to Kiseleva, Nov. 2, 1888; to Pleshcheyev, Jan. 15, 1889, he wrote: "My Bear is feeding me."

[63] Chekhov to Suvorin, May 4, 1889.

[64] Maeterlinck, "The Modern Drama," in *The Double Garden*, pp. 122-23.

Chekhov's disappointment was great when *The Wood Spirit* was unanimously rejected. His friend Pleshcheyev advised him to postpone writing plays, calling his talent "epic" (March 9, 1889). For seven long years he gave up the stage, although the search for a new dramatic form unceasingly occupied his mind. He meditated upon a realistic play, in which he could introduce a symbol as a means of communicating to the audience his inner and deeper thoughts.

An incident, unimportant in itself, furnished him with the symbol and at the same time gave him a theme for a complex, psychological drama. The painter Levitan, who lived in the neighborhood, once more in love, as usual attempted suicide. This time it was serious. No blood had been shed, however. The ladies whose guest he was, very much upset, sent for Chekhov, who arrived to find his friend with a tiny scratch on his forehead. It was more than he had expected. Laughingly he suggested a walk as the best remedy. Levitan, still clutching his gun, went along in the blackest mood. On the river bank he saw gulls flying and, as an emotional outlet, shot and killed one of them. The kind-hearted Chekhov, fond of every living thing, became indignant. In a letter to Suvorin (April 8, 1892) he described how the bird was shot and concluded: "Another beautiful, living creature is gone, but two dumbbells returned home and had supper."

Accused of unnecessary cruelty, Levitan threw the little bird at the feet of his beloved in a dramatic gesture, of which Chekhov made use in the second act of his play. Treplev in *The Sea Gull* says to Nina: "I had the meanness to kill that gull today. I place it at your feet." Trigorin (another character), seeing the dead bird, makes note of it in his book: "A theme occurred to me, a theme for a little sketch." *The Sea Gull*, inspired by this insignificant

incident, became a symbolic representation of the joyless
'90s, a logical continuation of the barren and melancholy
'80s. And Chekhov, who lived his intense inner life vicari-
ously, expressed through his characters his own thoughts.
"Life must be represented not as it is, but as it ought to
be, as it appears in dreams," says Treplev. And Doctor
Dorn agrees with him: "You chose your subject in the
realm of the abstract and you are quite right."

The final decade of the nineteenth century was the beginning of a new era in dramatic art — the creation of
mood — initiated by Maurice Maeterlinck, who was the
first to introduce *l'âme faible*, the weary soul of the *fin de
siècle*, "with paralysis of external action."[65] It was a search
for a new form of expression; "a lordly, passionate life"
was gone and the drama had to stand for the reality of
our time. Accidents and adventures exist no longer, but
the terrible unknown will be eternally with us. New problems have "been put forward as a substitute for the vast
enigma of the Providence or Fatality of the Old." The
modern drama stripped of visible action "has fallen back
on itself, and seeks to discover, in the regions of psychology and of moral problems, the equivalent of what once
was offered by exterior life."[66] It shows us conflicts between passion and a deep sense of moral law inherent in
all of us.

The dramas of Chekhov, with their peculiar structure,
corresponded exactly to the principles of the Belgian playwright except in that they conveyed to the spectator not

---

[65] *La Princesse Maleine*, 1889; *L'Intruse; Les Aveugles*, 1890; *Les Sept
Princesses*, 1891; *Péleas et Mélisande*, 1892; *L'Intérieur; La Mort de
Tintagiles; Alladine et Palomides*, 1894; *Aglavaine et Sélisette*, 1896.
Chekhov was extremely fond of the Belgian playwright and wrote to
Suvorin, July 12, 1897: "I am reading Maeterlinck — strange, peculiar
things, but the impression is tremendous."

[66] Maeterlinck, "The Modern Drama," in *The Double Garden*, pp. 118,
124, 125-26.

the feeling of terror created by Maeterlinck but a feeling of immobility and profound sadness. "The air is hot and still," says Irina Arkadina in *The Sea Gull*, and that peculiar stillness becomes the *leit-motif* about which is built the whole delicate symphony of this play. Its *dramatis personae* are no more than melancholy shadows, whose lives are merely delusion, a dream. "I have never lived, I have never had any experiences, but I want to live," exclaims the middle-aged Sorin. Nina, a young girl, almost a child, tells us also that she wants "to begin her life anew." Though they do not live, unseen tragedies lurk in the darkness for all of them. Their capacity for suffering is inversely proportional to their habitual apathy. The plot is extremely simple, as in all the plays of Chekhov. He is not interested in the past or the future of his characters but considers them for just one moment and at that particular moment presents their inner conflicts and hidden sorrows against the melancholy background of an autumnal setting.

Treplev, a penniless, dejected young man, writes a decadent play most distasteful to his mother, Irina Arkadina, a provincial actress and a mediocre, selfish woman, who is spending her summer on the estate of her brother, Sorin, in company with her lover, Trigorin. She is jealous of the young girl, Nina Sarechnaya, who is to act the leading role, and she humiliates her son by calling his work "decadent rubbish." Treplev loves Nina but feels that life holds no promise for him. He attempts suicide, but recovers and takes up again his drab existence.

Nina, for her part, is attracted to the writer Trigorin, whom she has idealized. He takes her with him, wrecks her life, and returns to his old mistress, Arkadina. It is like an endless chain of unhappy loves. Masha, daughter of the manager of the estate, loves Treplev and out of disappointment marries an insignificant schoolmaster. Her mother, Paulina Shamraeva, desperately loves the indifferent Doctor Dorn, who thinks that those tiresome people are under "the spell of the lake." In the fourth act, Nina, the little sea gull with broken wings, returns, almost insane after her unhappy adventure with Trigorin. Treplev, whom she still refuses, again attempts suicide and this time succeeds.

The main purpose of this delicate and tender play was to show the successive alterations of mood. Its lyrical character, strange and dreamlike; the new and peculiar form of the dialogue, inconsistent, inadequate, giving the impression that something of utmost importance has been hinted at but not said; odd pauses inserted to create a definite mood — the whole original structure, everything was a protest against the routine and the convention of the theatre.

Chekhov wrote to Suvorin, "It is a comedy with three feminine and six masculine roles, in four acts with a landscape (in sight of the lake), many conversations, little action, and two hundred pounds of love; I began it in *forte* and finished in *pianissimo*, contrary to all the rules of dramatic art. It turned out to be a novelette. I am more dissatisfied than contented and, upon reading my newborn comedy, am convinced once more that I am not a playwright."[67] Indeed, he realized somewhat uneasily that *The Sea Gull* would be incomprehensible to the general public. Accompanied by the writer Potapenko, he went every day to the rehearsals and tried to give the actors his directions, but no one listened to the inexperienced playwright.

The Sea Gull was presented on October 17, 1896 for the benefit of the actress Levkeyeva at the Alexandrine

[67] Chekhov to Suvorin, Nov. 10 and Nov. 21, 1895.

(Imperial) Theatre, which, like the *Comédie Française*, was the incarnation of old traditions. Levkeyeva, a well-known comedienne, attracted her own public, which came for amusement and laughter. It was startled by this strange "comedy." Poorly rehearsed, misunderstood by the directors, it proved a complete fiasco in spite of the excellent performances of Davydov, Varlamov and Vera Kommissarzhevskaya — all three famous actors of the time. The play within the play, in which Madame Kommissarzhevskaya recited the monologue of the "spirit of the universe," called by Arkadina "decadent rubbish," was met with an outburst of laughter. Kommissarzhevskaya continued courageously, but every moment it became more difficult to hear her in the din, hitherto unknown to the walls of the dignified Alexandrine Theatre. Treplev's quarrel with his mother increased the general hilarity, and soon whistles and shouts were heard from the orchestra and the gallery. The failure seemed complete and irreparable, even to the best friends of Chekhov. On the next day the reviews noted the "depressing effects of this morbid comedy and in its author a profound inner ailment." The literary enemies of Anton Pavlovich were overjoyed. His laurels, his ever-increasing fame, had irked many of his contemporaries. The negative verdict was unanimous, except for the faithful Suvorin, who in *Novoe Vremya* (October 17, 1896) defended him with the loyalty of a devoted friend and claimed that Chekhov had "a real dramatic talent."

On October 17 Suvorin recorded in his diary: "Merezhkovsky, whom I met in the theatre, said that the play was not intelligent, for the first quality of intelligence is clarity. I let him understand rather plainly that he never had that clarity himself." Yet we find later this curious entry: "*The Sea Gull* was given in the Alexandrine Theatre. It was unsuccessful. Chekhov is depressed. There are many faults, too little action. I was sure of the complete success of the play and wrote my review beforehand, but had to do it all over."

How much Suvorin liked Chekhov, how he believed in him and shielded him, is to be seen once more by the entry in his diary for October 21: "I am satisfied that I have written a note about *The Sea Gull* which is in opposition to everything said by others." Nevertheless, influenced by the general impression, he agreed that "the play was weak."

The *mood* and the artistic handling of reality were scarcely known at that time. The play seemed pretentious and irritated the critics as well as the public. Besides, the Russians of the '90s, brought up on discussions and debates, loved all kinds of "questions." These had to be raised in every respectable literary work and had to be answered by the author. Why do Nina and Treplev perish so pathetically? Why do the trivial Arkadina and Trigorin continue their selfish lives? Why is sorrow a predominant feature in human existence? Why? Why? Why? And Chekhov did not solve any of these problems.

Depressed, he fled hurriedly to Moscow. His sister remembers that the whole night after the performance he walked in a thin, penetrating drizzle through the cold streets of St. Petersburg, then caught the early train.

Anton Pavlovich was wise to leave. In the succeeding days all the comic papers pounced upon him, as his biographer, Izmailov, relates: "The Marabou cracked jokes and wrote funny rhymes in *Al'bom Svistunov* (The Album of Whistlers). *Shpil'ka* (The Pin) lyrically mourned the 'poor Russian stage, profaned by the criminal performance.' *Akula* (The Shark) deplored the failure of poor Mr. Chekhov and . . . the lost rubles of the public."

Many parodies appeared in verse and in prose. *The*

Sea Gull was called the "comedy in two shots with pro-
logue and epilogue, a subject taken from the insane
asylum."

Suvorin again magnanimously came forward in defense
of Chekhov. On October 19, 1896, he wrote in *Novoe
Vremya*: "This is the day of triumph for many newspapermen and writers. The comedy of the most gifted of the
young Russian authors was not successful — that is the
reason for the triumph. . . . Oh, story tellers and judges!
Who are you? What are your names and your merits?
I think Chekhov can sleep peacefully and work. . . . He
will remain in Russian literature with his outstanding
talent . . . you will only buzz and disappear."

As for Chekhov himself, he energetically protested
against the accusation concerning his flight. He wrote to
Suvorin on October 22: "In your last letter (October 18)
you thrice called me an old woman and said that I quailed.
Why this defamation? After the performance, I did honor
to my supper at Romanov's restaurant, then retired and
slept well, and the next day left for home without giving
utterance to any complaint . . . When you came to see
me the night after the performance, you said yourself that
the best thing would be to leave. . . . The next day I
received your letter bidding me farewell. Where, then, do
you see my cowardice? I acted coolly, like a man who has
proposed, been refused, and has nothing left to do but
to go."

In those days of discouragement and gloom, Chekhov
was not alone. Many friends besides Suvorin and Leikin
wrote him kind and sympathetic letters. He was especially
pleased with the attention of the famous jurist, Alexander
Fedorovich Koni, who was indignant with the unjust reception of *The Sea Gull* at the Alexandrine Theatre and

praised the idea of the "room with three walls," as Treplev (*The Sea Gull*, Act II) calls the stage.

Leo Tolstoy, however, was dissatisfied. He disliked the plays of Chekhov. Suvorin noted in his diary (February 11, 1897):

I visited Tolstoy, who has not been in Petersburg for twenty years. About *The Sea Gull* Lev Nikolaevich [Tolstoy] said: "This is nonsense, not worthy of anything, written as Ibsen writes. Words are piled up, and why, no one knows. And Europe shouts: 'Excellent!' Chekhov is certainly the most gifted of all, but *The Sea Gull* is very poor."

"Chekhov would die if he were told that you think so. Don't tell him."

"I shall do it, but kindly and I'll be surprised if he is vexed. Everyone has his weak points."

Chekhov, upon returning to Melikhovo, was so depressed that his sister and his friends promised themselves never to allow his plays to be produced again. At that time he wrote in his *Note-Books* (p. 67): "The sun shines, but my soul is in darkness." His health was rapidly declining. The walk in the drizzling rain in St. Petersburg on the cold October night had brought his illness to a climax. In the spring of 1897, after the publication of "The Peasants" he was forced to enter the private hospital of Professor Ostroumov. Thin, exhausted, with a bad cough and high fever, he arrived there in a very dangerous state. On March 24, Suvorin with his usual precision entered in his diary: "The day before yesterday Chekhov was taken ill as we went to dinner at the Hermitage. He asked for ice and we left without dinner." On March 26, he wrote: "Chekhov lies in No. 16, ten numbers higher than his 'Ward No. 6.'"

This stay in the hospital deprived Anton Pavlovich of his last illusions concerning his lungs. It was obvious that life in the North was henceforth impossible. In the lugubrious quiet of his room, he bitterly reproached himself that he, a physician, could have so unpardonably neglected his own health. For hours he remained motionless, brooding over his condition. From his bed he could see the ancient Novodevichii Convent, where two hundred years before, Peter the Great had forced his ambitious elder sister, Sophia Alexeyevna, to take the perpetual monastic vows (October 21, 1698). As Chekhov looked at its five cupolas sharply outlined against the sad, gray sky and heard its bells ringing for Vespers and for early Mass, as he watched the beginning of the timid northern spring and listened to the shrill voices of the boys playing their noisy games in the streets, he suddenly fell in love, hopelessly, desperately, with the same Moscow which a few years before had frightened even his imagination. Life was playing on him one of its bizarre jokes!

When he began to feel better, many of his friends came to see him. Tolstoy came and they walked along the corridor, talking of philosophy. It is recorded that the conversation was about the immortality of the soul. Chekhov remarked with his usual humor that Tolstoy, who had heard of his dangerous illness, expected to find him dying, and when he saw him not only alive but even improving, expressed on his face a sort of disappointment.

Shcheglov came frequently, and one day Anton Pavlovich said to him: "You know who sat here in that armchair? Tolstoy himself." Then he added: "With all my respect for Lev Nikolaevich [Tolstoy], I disagree with him on many, many questions." A terrible cough interrupted Chekhov's speech then. Shcheglov never learned on what points Chekhov disagreed with Tolstoy.[68] Perhaps he was referring to that conversation on immortality — a subject

[68] Shcheglov's recollections, in *Niva*, June, 1905.

OLD MOSCOW

which always stirred Chekhov, who feared annihilation. His thoughts often dwelt on death. Like many Russians, he considered it an exciting mystery, never to be unravelled on earth, its solution attainable only in physical destruction. Sometimes he hoped that faith would give the long-desired peace to his restless mind, sometimes he accepted as a pantheist the existence of an impersonal, universal soul. Suvorin reports in his diary Chekhov's thoughts about death: "Death is a cruel, horrible execution. There is no life in the beyond if, after death, individuality is annihilated. I cannot be consoled with the idea that I shall become one with the sighs and the sufferings of the universal soul, which may perhaps have a goal, but to me even the goal is unknown."

What his real thoughts on that subject were, no one knew. In the final analysis, however, it seems that Chekhov remained a skeptic. On July 12, 1903, he wrote to Sergey Diagilev, editor of the outstanding periodical *Mir Iskusstva* (The World of Art) and famous promoter of the Russian ballet: "Long ago I lost my faith; it is with perplexity that I look upon religious people among the intelligentsia."

After Chekhov left the hospital, Suvorin suggested a trip to Western Europe, but in vain. Anton Pavlovich preferred to stay near his beloved Moscow as long as the weather was warm. He knew that he would have to spend his future winters in the South. Suvorin recorded in his diary: "I couldn't persuade Chekhov to go with me. He said that in the fall he had planned to go to Korfu . . . to Malta, where he would translate Maupassant. He likes him very much."

Chekhov never translated Maupassant, but he had already in 1894 drawn the attention of the reading public to the French master by causing a character in his story

"Women Folk" to speak these lines: "Maupassant . . . a wonderful writer, an excellent writer. As an artist he is extraordinary! What a tremendous, colossal, superhuman writer! Every line opens a new horizon to you. The delicate and tender movements of the soul are succeeded by strong and stormy emotions. . . . What richness of transitions, melodies, and motifs! . . . What irresistible, beautiful, powerful thoughts!"

In 1897, when Chekhov hoped to begin his translation, Maupassant, already dead for four years, was universally acknowledged as a master in France, highly appreciated by Tolstoy, and enthusiastically read in Russia. At that time, the clouds, though still thick, were slowly dispersing on the literary horizon. In a few years Russia was to enter a period of artistic renascence. The road was to a great extent paved by Chekhov, the innovator, who like Maupassant, had no rival in his own literary field.

In the fall Anton Pavlovich was persuaded to go to the Riviera. He went, not as a traveler, but as an invalid in search of sunshine. His journey was dull and uneventful; he felt again the pangs of distress. Chekhov was not particularly attracted by Western Europe. Timid, he was especially ill at ease with the lively French. Therefore his first impulse was to seek the society of his compatriots. From the letter to Suvorin (October 11, 1897) we learn that he was living in Nice in a Russian boardinghouse: "It is warm here, the sea is tender and caressing. The Promenade des Anglais is fresh and green . . . I met Maxim Kovalevsky, a former professor at Moscow University. It is so easy and pleasant to be with him."

Fate, indeed, was kind to Chekhov in bringing into his life many brilliant people of his epoch. Maxim Maximovich Kovalevsky (1851-1916), a charming man and a great scholar, was a professor of sociology and history. Expelled from the university of Moscow for his ultra-radical ideas, he had founded in Paris a school of social science (1901) where Lenin and Plekhanov taught. At the time when he met Anton Pavlovich, he was living in his villa on the Riviera. In the following fragment of his diary which has never before been published he gives us his impressions of Chekhov.

Chekhov, who came often to see me in my villa at Beaulieu when he was living in the Russian boardinghouse at Nice (Rue Gounaud), made an impression completely unlike that of Merezhkovsky. He had a broad and healthy mind developed by the study of natural science, distinguished by keen observation, wit, and the capacity for noticing characteristic traits of people and representing them with artistic simplicity. He had not a trace of so-called philosophical training, nor of the many-sidedness of Turgenev or Tolstoy. Neither did he possess the humor of Gogol — the laughter with unseen, unnoticed tears under its surface — which strikes one not only in *Dead Souls* but also in tales like "The Cloak." Chekhov could by no means be called a satirist of the type of Saltykov [Shchedrin], with his burlesque. Chekhov's tales present in minute detail the Philistinism of the epoch of Russian stagnation. As for his own philosophy, I wouldn't say he had any. His attitude towards those things called in Russia the *burning questions* was indefinite. Whoever tried to find it out received from him rather elementary answers.

Chekhov's "The Peasants" presents perhaps the deepest of his literary themes. It was a criticism of the populist conception of desirable conditions in Russian villages. I am not surprised that the critics of *Russian Wealth* attacked it in wrath. "The Peasants" certainly hit their sensitive spot.

Chekhov was very conscientious towards his writing. He had even slighter inventive capacity than Turgenev . . . Chekhov loved the medical profession and readily extended his assistance to poor peasants. Everything concerning rural Russia interested him. Questions of political organization and parliamentarianism left him quite indifferent, yet he was an ardent partisan of such a social order as would permit everyone to live in peace with his own conscience. During the well-known Dreyfus affair he read newspapers with ardor. Convinced of the innocence of the "calumniated Jew," he wrote Suvorin in burning letters that it was dishonest to persecute an innocent man. Suvorin, as Chekhov told me, in answer to one of those letters wrote him: "You have convinced me." Yet never, added Chekhov, did *Novoe Vremya* fall with greater spite on the wretched captain than in the weeks and months following these letters. "How do you explain this?" I asked. "As nothing else," answered Chekhov, "than complete lack of backbone in Suvorin. I do not know a man more undecided, even in the questions pertaining to his family."

In Nice Chekhov was bored, as he would have been bored anywhere outside of Russia. He felt somewhat more animated in the society of the writers who arrived on the Riviera. With many of them he was quite intimate. In the days following the paroxysms of his illness Chekhov was gloomy and silent. A good physician, he did not delude himself with the hope of possible recovery but predicted that he would die relatively young.

Obliged to spend the winters in a warm climate, he strove to leave Nice for Algiers or Rome. He dared not risk a long voyage alone. I was free for several weeks. Together with Korotnev, I consented to accompany him. We never reached Algiers because of a bad storm in Marseilles. Then we turned back and traveled uninterruptedly to Florence, where Chekhov received the proof sheets of his play *The Three Sisters*. He spent the whole day reading them, was very much dissatisfied, and said gloomily that he would not write for the theatre any more. But that was only a passing mood. After *The Three Sisters* followed, as is known, *Uncle Vanya*.[69] In the production at the Art Theatre the plays of Chekhov had great success. He could not sufficiently praise this group of art lovers, led by Vl. I. Nemirovich-Danchenko. They had in their circle such artists "by the grace of God" as Alexeyev (Stanislavsky).

In Rome Chekhov showed his indifference as much to the antique monuments as to the medieval. On the first day of

[69] Here Professor Kovalevsky errs. *Uncle Vanya* preceded *The Three Sisters* by three years.

Lent we saw the procession at St. Peter's Cathedral, for the purpose of eradicating the spirit of carnival. When we came out I asked Chekhov: "How would you describe this procession in your tales?" "What is there to say about it?" he answered. "A stupid procession was dragged out." Chekhov was equally indifferent to the Forum, the Capitol, the ruins of the Imperial Palace on the Palatine. After two or three days, Rome lost all its charm for him, and he began to talk about his departure for Russia. We tried to change his mind, but in vain.

The following unpublished letter of Chekhov addressed to Professor Maxim Kovalevsky was found with the memoirs of the latter:

O fallacem hominem spem![70] Your letter, dear Maxim Maximovich, greatly saddened me, because I was raving about Algiers and dreamt every night that I was eating dates. I am so sorry that you are ill; seemingly your life in Paris is none too pleasant. From what illness are you suffering? Rheumatism or gout or both? The best thing for you, I believe, would be to come to Beaulieu and enjoy the warm springlike sun.

I am bored! My work goes slowly, lazy Little Russian that I am. I rarely go to Monte Carlo and have not gambled for a long time. It fatigues me physically to stand in that heat and melt.

Korotnev arrived. Turasov was ill. He had kidney trouble. This is the only news. Our *Pension Russe* is filled with people.

I am certainly flattered that "My Life"[71] was translated. At the moment (i. e., on the evening of January 20) I have none of my books. Tomorrow I shall go to dear old Mordukhai Rozanov to secure a volume that contains "My Life," if he has one, and I shall send it to you at once.

I have mailed a story to *Cosmopolis* [a periodical]. The publisher expressed his gratitude to me by wire, though I believe the story is weak.

[70] Chekhov puts the same expression in the mouth of Kulygin in *The Three Sisters*.

[71] "Moya Zhizn" (My Life), a story written much under the influence of Leo Tolstoy.

You, who are interested in the Russian economic situation, will probably be pleased to learn about an important new enactment in the domain of agriculture: last December the Rural Statistics Department invented a new badge for its correspondents! That is all!

The evenings are cold, but during the day the weather is wonderful. Do write me when you are coming.

Best wishes for your good health and a cordial handshake.

Yours,

A. Chekhov.

Ivanukov, as I have learned, apparently has tuberculosis. He is in the hospital.

The memoirs of Professor Maxim Kovalevsky are particularly interesting in that they give us at first hand the opinion of a man of rare intelligence. They fit perfectly with the description of Chekhov by all those who knew him closely. All unanimously praised his brilliant, unprejudiced mind, his great literary gifts. But all noticed at the same time his indifference and his restlessness, which can be explained by the fact that he, as a physician, realized his incurable illness and lived in a permanent horror of death.

In this comparative freedom, when he wrote very little, Anton Pavlovich began to be more attentive to political and social questions, on account of which he had been often persecuted by Mikhailovsky. The Dreyfus Affair stirred him so deeply that he thought about it long after it happened. "We talk of nothing here but of Zola and Dreyfus. The immense majority of educated people believe, with Zola, that Dreyfus was innocent. Zola has gained immensely in public esteem. His letters of protest [Chekhov meant Zola's famous *J'accuse*] are like a breath of fresh air."[72]

The sensational Dreyfus trial, which excited all France

[72] Chekhov to Batushkov, Jan. 28, 1898.

[132]

fallacem hominum spem! [handwritten Russian text, illegible] дорогой ... Максимович, меня весьма огорчил, ибо ... , в среднем ... и мне картины моей ... , а той финики, ... в городе, досадно, что Вы больше ... , повидимому, в Париж ... Вам не весело. Кто ... Вас? Ревнуете, ... Что ж, ... другие будут! ... сожалею, что сейчас бы весь Вам ... ... в ... ... и ... на солнце, которое ... ... на ...

... . Работал было, как ...

FIRST PAGE OF A LETTER FROM CHEKHOV TO KOVALEVSKY

and the ever-responsive Russia, played an important role in the personal life of Chekhov, for it apparently caused the break with his old friend, Suvorin, who adhered to the official version and fulminated against the "traitor" in the pages of *Novoe Vremya*. Chekhov, on the other hand, took the side of the accused captain and, especially, of Zola, who came out in defense of Dreyfus. In great excitement he wrote to Suvorin (February 6, 1898): "You say that Zola is vexing you, but all of us here have the feeling that a better Zola is born. He has shown a purity and a moral height which no one suspected. Indeed Zola is not Voltaire, but there are times when the reproach that we are not Voltaires is not appropriate.[73] Even supposing Dreyfus is guilty, Zola is still right, since the duty of the writer is not to accuse or prosecute, but to intercede for the culprits when they suffer penalties."

To his brother Alexander he wrote (February 23, 1898): "In the case of Zola, *Novoe Vremya* behaved abominably. On this account the *old man* and I exchanged letters and both became silent. I do not wish to write him nor do I wish to receive his letters."

It is hard to see how Chekhov, gentle and indifferent, could break with an old and tried friend on account of persons strange to both of them. Is it that Anton Pavlovich began to dislike the tendencies of *Novoe Vremya* which he had disregarded in his youth? The fact is that he showed unusual irritation towards Suvorin. This point is a delicate one for the student of Chekhov who wants to maintain a complete impartiality, yet it is quite essential. Chekhov with great ease left Leikin, whom he called at one time his "godfather," before he met Alexey Su-

---

[73] Chekhov probably alludes to the famous *Affaire Calas* in Toulouse. Calas was executed March 10, 1762. Voltaire, sure of his innocence, tried to rehabilitate his memory and succeeded after three years of fighting.

vorin. He also rapidly cooled towards Grigorovich. It seems as though deep feelings of personal friendship were impossible to this limp soul.

Was it that Suvorin, healthy and strong, with his monopolizing friendship fatigued the sick and nervous Anton Pavlovich? Was it because new interests or affections sundered him from his old friend? It does not seem that Suvorin at first realized Chekhov's estrangement. To all of those who have read Suvorin's diary, his deep and sincere friendship for Chekhov is evident. "No matter through what prism one looks at the role of Suvorin in the life of Chekhov, it is beautiful. Suvorin adored Chekhov, and never required any compromises with *Novoe Vremya*," wrote Amfiteatrov, one of Chekhov's contemporaries who had many opportunities to see them together. "Doubtless Suvorin influenced Chekhov in his literary development. How could this be otherwise? Suvorin was a highly educated, talented old writer with an excellent memory, a brilliant stylist endowed with a sure taste. And Suvorin has generously said that he owed much to Chekhov, to this beautiful soul who rejuvenated him. He claimed that there was something new in Chekhov, as if he came from another life, another world."[74]

During the spring of 1898, however, the two friends saw each other frequently. In Suvorin's diary (April 27) there is a note: "Chekhov is here [in Paris]. He is with me all the time." With his usual precision he relates that the populist circles were attacking Chekhov's "The Peasants" for overcoloring and exaggeration, and he energetically concludes: "True asses are these men, who understand less of literature than do pigs of oranges, yet these pigs permit themselves to judge the most outstanding writer." It does not seem that Suvorin changed. Friendship for

[74] Izmailov, pp. 467-69.

him was more than a passing fancy. But not so for Chekhov, who wrote to Nemirovich-Danchenko (December 3, 1899): "He and I do not correspond any more."

From that time indeed the correspondence almost ceased. The last letter of Chekhov, short and casual, dated July 1, 1903, concerned his colleague, Doctor Veresaev. "I read Veresaev's stories and think you will be very much pleased with them. Veresaev is a physician. I got to know him lately and he makes a very good impression."

This separation, although definite, was peaceful. There were no storms in the life of the gentle Chekhov. "We separate peacefully, as we lived peacefully. As long as my books were printed in your publishing house, we never had any misunderstanding," he wrote to Suvorin in 1899. So indifferently and easily were severed the ties with a man whose tactful protection and stimulating influence had guided him for thirteen long years. Strange Chekhov! It would, indeed, seem that he did come from another world!

X

Crimean Banishment

I, MY dear man, do not understand life and I fear it; I don't know; perhaps I am sick and crazy. A normal and healthy person feels that he understands everything that he sees and hears. But I have lost that feeling and day after day I poison myself with fear. There is a trouble called the fear of space; I am troubled with the fear of life."[75]

The exasperating, and at the same time alluring, mirage called life had always enchanted Chekhov, the tired wanderer, who ardently wished to live, but had never learned the secret of living. Tuberculosis riveted him to Yalta, a charming spot on the Black Sea, surrounded with gardens and an amphitheatre of mountains that protected it from the cold winds of the steppes. Famous for its beauty as well as for its historical past, the Crimean Peninsula has always attracted the traveler. Ruins of ancient Greek settlements (Tauric Chersonese), Genoese watchtowers, remains of the palaces of the Ottoman Turks, all the exotic, colorful world from Ai-Todor to Bakhchisaray, which once inspired Pushkin to write *The Fountain of Backchisaray*, was wasted on Chekhov, who saw in it merely a health resort. The "green faces" of its inhabitants made

[75] "Strakh" (Fear, 1892).

him hate it as a reminder of his own illness. His imagination was quick to adorn the distant Melikhovo with all the charm of the Arabian Nights. Alone and forlorn, he wandered from hotel to hotel, displeased with their discomforts and with his own indolence, which was becoming more and more his natural state of mind until the sudden death of his father (October 12, 1898) called him back to reality.

Chekhov was never attached to his father. The childhood of the sensitive boy had been darkened by punishments, by stern and joyless piety, by perpetual attendance at church, and by the singing of endless hymns. He could not forget the vulgarity of the grocery store and the hard years of his youth. In his numerous letters, which fill many a volume, there is not one addressed to his father. Yet Chekhov was deeply shaken by this death. All his life he had made a cult of his family. A swarm of memories now filled his mind. It was sweet and yet distressing to think of bygone days, of the distant past, always so attractive, always surrounded by a glow. The cycle of Melikhovo was ended. "It seems to me that now Father is dead, there will be no life in Melikhovo," he wrote to his sister on October 12, 1898.

The necessity of remaining in the South compelled Chekhov to build a new home in Yalta, a quaint white dwelling enclosed by a flower garden, beyond which lay an abandoned Moslem cemetery. This house stood on a promontory. Its windows overlooked blue water sparkling in the sun, but the eternal magic of the sea no longer cast a spell over this weary soul, now sunk in a drowsiness for which the only remedy was permanent change. And soon, very soon, the gentle Chekhov began once more to grumble: "Here even the bacilli sleep. I am bored and am turning into a narrow-minded provincial. I think I shall fall in love with a pock-marked female who will beat me on week-days and on holidays pity me."[76]

Chekhov's boredom was less explicable than ever, for he was surrounded by the most famous men of Russia, who visited the Crimea during the years he lived there. Tolstoy, Rachmaninov, Gorky, Kuprin, and Bunin were certainly brilliant and stimulating. Yet nothing could lift Chekhov's mind from the deepening shadow of death.

One day, as he sat on the bench in the square, the writer, Bunin, asked him, "Do you like the sea, Anton Pavlovich?"

"Yes" he answered, "only it is too barren. . . . I think it is wonderful to be an army officer or a young student, to sit somewhere in a crowded place and listen to music."

This unexpected transition from the sea to the officer, Bunin surmises, "was doubtless called forth by a hidden sadness about youth and health. . . . He loved life and joy and longed for happiness."[77]

The financial affairs of Anton Pavlovich were in a state of complete chaos, naturally increasing his feeling of discomfort and insecurity. He began to consider seriously the stabilization of his income by publishing a complete edition of his works. Tolstoy, a great admirer of his short stories, tried to help him. He said to Sergeyenko, Chekhov's school friend: "Tell Marks that I urgently request him to publish Chekhov. After Turgenev and Goncharov, he has nothing left to do but publish Chekhov and me. But Chekhov is much more interesting than we old fellows."[78]

Spurred on by Tolstoy, in the ennui of his Yalta exile, Chekhov began the heavy task of revising his voluminous

---

[76] Chekhov to Tikhonov-Lugovoy, writer and editor of the periodical *Siever* (The North).

[77] Bunin, V, 293.

[78] Sergeyenko's recollections in *Niva*, Oct., 1904. Marks was a well-known publisher in St. Petersburg.

work. He was severe with himself and often discarded the early stories of Antosha Chekhonte. The result of this labor soon appeared in the collected edition of his tales, which encompassed so many phases of human tragedy and disclosed the evils that were to bring Russia to the greatest of all revolutions. It may be said that Chekhov's pessimism lay not only in his own character but also in the impressions of a medical man who studied the process of life with scientific precision and, as an impartial witness, drew a true picture of what he had seen around him.

The writings of Anton Pavlovich fall into three distinct groups, according to the people with whom they deal — with children, with peasants, with the intelligentsia — all treated with perfect objectivity, without favorites or heroes, yet permeated with love and sympathy, especially noticeable in his stories about children. With the tenderness inherited from his mother, he knew how to approach the child and to understand his psychology. He realized that childhood is an independent period of human life, having its own special values. In his *Note-Books* are to be found several charming bits about children: "a little girl with rapture about her aunt — 'She is very beautiful, as beautiful as our dog.' . . . 'Mama! What is a thunderbolt made of?' . . . 'Mama! Don't show yourself to the guests, you are very fat!' "[79]

Chekhov cherished children. With his usual keenness of observation, he noticed the negative side of Russian life, the lack of systematic upbringing, the misunderstanding which might scar those young beings for life. He pitied them deeply, saw their privation and misery, their abandonment by selfish parents, who in a truly Russian fashion dreamed about a beautiful but remote future and indolently forgot their immediate tasks.

[79] Chekhov, *Note-Books*, pp. 33, 51, 67.

Crimean Banishment

In Russian literature from Dostoyevsky on, there was a tendency to present tortured little creatures — "Netochka Nesvanova," Nellie (*Humiliated and Offended*), the children of Katherina Ivanovna (*Crime and Punishment*) — all victims of hysterical or poverty-stricken parents. To the same category belong the charming story of Korolenko, *In Bad Society,* the heartbreaking *Village* of Grigorovich, and Gorky's nightmarish *Childhood.*

Tolstoy alone represented the happy children of the upper classes, in pleasant surroundings. As for Chekhov, his sense of truth and his simplicity of narrative method enabled him to paint the sufferings of children with especial force in stories like "Van'ka" and "Sleepy." But he also knew how to depict the happiness and the light-heartedness of the first years of their lives; he reproduced their speech, their characters, their kindness, their quarrels and sorrows, and their surprise at the strange new world about them.

In "The Cook's Wedding," the seven-year-old Grisha is startled when the family cook, Pelageya, who has lived peacefully and happily by herself, suddenly decides to marry an enormous and — to the little boy — terrifying coachman. Grisha is quite sure that Pelageya is frightened too. In order to express his profound sympathy for her, he brings her the largest apple from the pantry, confident that it will greatly console her.

In "The Boys," we watch with interest the twelve-year-old Chechevitzin, who is not a Russian boy at all, but Montihomo, the Hawk Claw, the invincible leader of an Indian tribe. This victim of Captain Mayne Reid persuades his friend, the fat little Volodya, "the pale face," to run away to California instead of spending a dull Christmas at home. The voyage will be very simple. They have only to reach Bering Strait, from which America is but a stone's throw. Equipped with one penknife and a few sandwiches, the boys escape by night, but they are soon caught by the police, to the despair of Montihomo and the secret joy of Volodya, who is happy to return to his dog, his sisters, and his Christmas tree.

In "The Children" there is a description of five tiny creatures who play lotto with much zeal. They quarrel, slap each other, and cry, but are immediately reconciled, and their little faces, still covered with tears, are once more suffused with happiness and joy.

Chekhov's children are mostly confident and easy-going, quickly responsive to kindness on the part of grownups. Pashka, a seven-year-old peasant boy whose arm is about to be amputated, is very much frightened when he first comes to the hospital. He tries to run away but is brought back and soon makes friends with a kind doctor, who promises to show him a living fox. Pashka is enchanted and forgets his fears ("The Fugitive"). All the works of the author are permeated with sympathy and love for the small and unprotected. The delightful "Kashtanka" is the story of a dog, told in the first person.[80] Kashtanka is picked up in the street by a circus clown, who teaches her many tricks, while a small boy, the son of a carpenter, mourns the loss of his only companion. At a performance of the circus the child recognizes Kashtanka and shouts with excitement. The dog, forgetting her good manners, leaps over the heads of the spectators to join her little master and the two friends are happily reunited.

Children, as Chekhov shows us, have their own psychology. In the story "At Home," an intelligent and thoughtful father sees with amusement that his six-year-

[80] "Kashtanka" was very popular with Suvorin's children. Chekhov wrote to his brother Mikhail (March 15, 1888): "The children incessantly gaze at me and expect me to say something very intelligent. In their opinion I am a genius, since I have written the story about Kashtanka."

old son, whom he wants to punish for misbehavior (smoking), answers all arguments with his own logic.

In all these exquisite short tales of two or three pages we see many young beings so masterfully drawn that they all keep their distinctive traits. We share their happiness in "The Children," or experience their sorrow, as in "Trifles" or "Superfluous People," in which tender, innocent souls meet with human vulgarity for the first time. Together with Chekhov, we love all of them, the rich, "slender-limbed in velvet suits," and the poor, "with ears sticking out and little iron crosses on their chests."[81]

As an objective writer, Chekhov often stirred up questions that aroused the attention of the reading public. When he depicted Russian peasants and the hardship and the coarseness of village life, he invariably provoked criticism from the populist group. The peasant question, the big question in Russia, was discussed by many writers and sociologists. For some of them, the peasants were pathetic and ignorant beings who had to be enlightened; others again idealized them, believing them to be bearers of mysterious, unknown truth which they alone could reveal.

Chekhov approached the peasants in a new way. In showing them just as they were, he displayed once more his sharp and analytic mind. His pictures are often as gloomy as Maupassant's, except that now and then there are bright spots, showing, in truly Chekhovian manner, some hope for a better future ("The New Country Home"). The intelligentsia have to learn the peasant psychology in order to help them, and Chekhov strikingly illustrates the gulf which separates the two classes ("The Darkness"). He does not moralize or pass judgment; he

---

[81] "Children." It is customary in the Eastern Church to receive at baptism a cross, which is worn throughout one's life. The poor people wear iron crosses, which have become a symbol of poverty.

simply presents facts of tragic misunderstanding and ignorance.

In "The Catastrophe," Avdeyev, condemned for defalcation, does not know how it happened and thinks that he is the victim of a plot. "The Malefactor" depicts an ignorant peasant who unconsciously becomes a criminal. That unscrewing the nuts from railroad ties (to use as sinkers for his fishing) could cause an accident never enters his mind. Sent to jail, he sincerely believes that there is an error: "What! To jail! But I have no time. I must go to the fair!"

Like Maupassant, Chekhov analyzes the dim, hazy minds of the peasants, their distrust, their prejudices, even towards those who are kind to them. He shows the very depth of stupidity and cruelty in scenes which become almost prophetic in their description of the destructive instincts of the Russian people. This coarseness and primitive psychology are best delineated in his two most accomplished stories, which, besides his usual mastery and penetration, show great power and stand apart from all the rest of his work. These are "Mujiki" (The Peasants, 1897) and "V Ovragie" (In the Ravine, 1901), both suggested by his life in Melikhovo.

One can only marvel with what art he presents in the twenty-six pages of the first story a situation that involves the whole mass of the peasantry. There is not to be found in Russian literature another example of such a tremendous social problem exposed with equal conciseness and strength. After many years spent in the capital where he has had glimpses of refined life, Nikolay, a waiter in a large Moscow hotel, falls ill and returns to his native village with his wife and daughter, Olga and Sasha. At home they are struck by the filth and the rudeness of the peasants, "who live worse than cattle" in hard daily labor, dimly aware of the aimless flight of life. "The old people thought how beautiful youth was . . . in the darkness two windows fully lighted by the moon, the silence, the squeak of the cradle reminded them strangely that life had gone and would never more return." In these lyrical, sad words one finds the ever-recurrent *leit-motif* of Chekhov, regretful sorrow, later masterfully developed in *The Three Sisters*. Daily the former waiter sees drunkenness, laziness, and abject poverty. He is repelled by his old mother, who in her stinginess and her evil character seems utterly to lack human qualities. His drunken brother beats his unresponsive wife almost to death. Thekla, stupid, sensual, the worthy spouse of the second brother, often spends nights in abominable orgies and the next day, too lazy to work, makes life miserable for Nikolay, Olga, and little Sasha. Here again we meet Chekhov's constant theme, the suffering of the innocent through the cruel, a thesis so artfully maintained by Henry James in some of his works.[82] Finally Nikolay dies from lack of food and care. The two luminous figures of Olga and Sasha stand out from that dark, sinister background. They leave the inhospitable house and stray through Russia as wanderers, never losing their faith and hope, fearing neither life nor death.

"In the Ravine," with a precision and tenseness that provoke feelings almost of physical pain — as in the works of Dostoyevsky — Chekhov describes the horror of a factory village, making it symbolic of darkness and cruelty. The wicked Aksinia, "a viper," with her small head and her slender body clad in a green dress, throws boiling water over her baby nephew, the only heir to the property, and chases Lipa, the child's mother, out of the house.

[82] *The Princess Casamassima, Daisy Miller, An International Episode.*

In contrast to her, the timid Lipa is "pale, thin, and frail," and looks like a "lark."

The parents-in-law, Gregory and Barbara, are weak old people. They cannot resist Aksinia, who has seized all power in the household. She exemplifies again the triumph of evil over good. The gentle Lipa and her frightened mother leave the rich house without protest. In them Chekhov shows that in the depths of the Russian heart there lies a profound indifference to the riches of earth. With small bundles of their miserable belongings on their backs, alone and unprotected, the two women go into the unknown world and meet some other wanderers whom they believe to be saints. Their conversation with these old men is a masterpiece of Russian literature. Lipa relates to them the last tortures of her murdered baby. There is no hatred in her innocent soul, only a deep surprise at so much wickedness and injustice. She surrenders to her fate like Olga and Sasha, admirable in her moral superiority despite her apparent weakness. Chekhov personified in all of them the religious mind of the Russians. He acknowledges that if the people had an ethical understanding of life it was on the basis of the Christian faith, in which he himself saw the law of higher morality. Those two profound stories are keyed in tone with the ideals of *Holy Russia* propounded by the Slavophils in the '40s. The concept of Holy Russia is very old; it originated in the faith that Moscow was the Third Rome and went back to the downfall of Constantinople (1453). The marriage of the Tsar Ivan III on November 12, 1472 to Sophia Paleologue, niece of the last emperor, Constantine XII, showed the strong bond between Moscow and the disintegrated Byzantine Empire. The theorists on Russian sovereignty in the sixteenth century, believed that the rightful successors of the Christian

Caesars of Byzantium were the Tsars, "the natural champions"[83] of the Eastern Church, and that their people — *the bearers of God* — had a great mission to fulfill among other nations. This idea soon had wide currency. It touched a sensitive chord in the hearts of Russians, "the sombre and mysterious children of destiny,"[84] who, detached from reality, disdained the pleasures and the joys of the earth and regarded the renunciation of personal happiness as a normal procedure. They believed that Russia had to be crucified for the sins of the world and considered her sufferings as the highest atonement.

Yet out of this sorrow and despair was to emerge a new dawn of brotherhood of man. Mother Russia was to become a new and enlightened leader. Constantine Leontiev, who, in contrast to the nihilists of the '60s, loved in the Russian people their deep faith and their Christian submissiveness, thoroughly disapproved of the bourgeois civilization of Western Europe with its devastating materialism. He saw in the faithfully kept traditions of Byzantium, in the sublime prayers and the detachment of the Eastern Church, a true expression of the spirit of Christianity as opposed to the pettiness of the West.[85] He pointed out the unavoidable bankruptcy of socialism on the ground that, sooner or later, the human genius would rebel against standardization. Therefore, in his brilliant and terse article, "Suum Cuique,"[86] he expressed his yearning for the attainment of the national "cultural

[83] Pares, *History of Russia*, p. 98: "After Constantinople had fallen into the hands of the Turks, John III took the title of the Sovereign of all Russia, also that of Tsar, or Caesar. Moscow claimed to be the third and the last Rome."

[84] Leontiev, "Vizantia i Slavianstvo" (Byzantium and Slavdom), in *Vostok, Rossia i Slavianstvo* (Orient, Russia, and Slavdom), V, 144.

[85] In France Vicomte de Bonald and Joseph de Maistre, like Leontiev, believed that the only salvation for their country lay in Catholicism.

[86] Leontiev, "Suum Cuique," in *Vostok, Rossia i Slavianstvo*, in his complete works, VI, 114.

renascence" and hoped to see "the golden cross on Saint Sophia above the blue waters of the majestic Thracean Bosphorus," thus voicing the eternal dream of the Russians — the conquest of Constantinople. He wanted to let the noisy, rattling train of the West pass Russia and agreed with the Slavophils that "Western Europe was in decay."[87] Fifty years later the ideas of Constantine Leontiev, which remained unnoticed in his own time, were repeated by Oswald Spengler in his *Untergang des Abendlandes* (The Decline of the West).

As for Chekhov, his art always reflected the tendencies and currents of Russian life. His dissatisfaction with his own time is best shown in depicting the tragedy of the Russian intelligentsia, who saw no way of eradicating, or even neutralizing, the ugliness and stagnation of that epoch. Therefore, the greater part of his writing bears the imprint of fatality. In depicting the intelligentsia, he showed not only the dreadful impasse of mutual misunderstanding, but the complete and hopeless solitude of the individual soul. People meet and pass each other without even noticing the distressing loneliness that is their common lot. Impressionable and gentle, they are hurt by common triviality but they suffer from "paralysis of the soul." Either they perish or else they become selfish and in turn make others suffer ("The Tale of the Unknown Man," "The Kiss"). His unheroic heroes fail to give proper value to the events of their existence or to the people who surround them. So Julia Sergeevna understands that she has enjoyed a great happiness only when it is gone ("Three Years"). Olga Ivanovna Dymova ("The Flippant"), always in search of a hero, realizes that her own husband was a really worthwhile man only

[87] Leontiev, "Zapiski Otshel'nika" (Memoirs of an Anchorite), in *Vostok, Rossia i Slaviansto*, in his complete works, VI, 103.

after his death. In the story called "The Wife," a married couple, good and intelligent, spend their lives together in a perpetual misunderstanding.

It would seem that a single word would clear this storm-laden atmosphere. But Chekhov's characters never say that word. Therefore, a simple, unimportant conflict grows and grows until it bursts out into a real catastrophe. And yet they all love life, "that incomprehensible, aimless joke," and, lulled by Maya, the ever-present illusion, eternally hope for a better future. Hope is, with them, an almost physiological capacity. Sometimes his charming misfits express high and beautiful thoughts. Ivan Ivanovich Shamokhin, who wrecks his life and ruins his father for a pretty but shallow woman ("Ariadna," 1895), after going through the humiliating sufferings of a carnal and giddy love, says: "I should like to think that the conquering human genius tried to overcome physical love like an enemy and, if he did not succeed in doing so, he, nevertheless, covered it with a veil of illusions, brotherhood, and love, and, for me at least, it is not only a simple animal function as in a dog or in a frog, but a real love when each embrace is a pure, spiritual, reverent transport of the heart."

If Ariadna is cold and calculating, not worthy of any sympathy or love, other women are no better. They are depraved and insignificant. Volodya the Younger can only despise Sophia L'vovna when she throws herself upon him. She is nothing in his life but a passing fancy. With her husband, Volodya the Elder, he has long and serious conversations. Irritated when she asks him to talk to her in the same way, he says ironically: "What do you want? Constitutional rights or sturgeon with horse radish?" He leaves her after one week of a most degrading love affair. And Sophia L'vovna, in hysterics, accepts all the care and all the money that her old husband can give her. Just as unattractive is Maniusya, the wife in "The Teacher of Literature," who reveals herself after her marriage as stingy, narrow, and stupid.

In general, Chekhov has not very much patience with women and severely criticizes them for the mischief and disorder they create in the lives of their husbands or lovers. Men, weak as they are, at least have their professions. They work, they strive towards higher ideals and provoke deep compassion for their sufferings. Women suffer only because they are idle and selfish. The chaste and moral Chekhov in the story entitled "Disaster"[88] does not sympathize with the wife of the notary public, Lubiantseva, who neglects her duties as woman and mother because her overworked and tired husband cannot take her away from her too enterprising admirer. Yet Chekhov never loses his most charming traits — his justice and his tenderness. He implies that if these women had been brought up by better parents in a better environment, they certainly would have been better. So we see Gurov, who believes with Schopenhauer that women are "lower beings" until he meets in Crimea the "Lady with the Dog," young, unaffected, attractive, and Gurov feels that "something big" has for the first time entered his life.

Anton Chekhov, as if redeeming his somewhat harsh attitude towards the fair sex, depicts young girls with remarkable gentleness. The charming figures of Sasha (*Ivanov*), Zhenya ("The House with a Mezzanine"), Nina (*The Sea Gull*), Sonya (*Uncle Vanya*), and Anya (*The Cherry Garden*) are all like little birds. With their wings soon to be broken, they stand, pure and innocent, at the threshold of a life which will brutally destroy their frail illusion of happiness.

[88] "Neschast'e" (Disaster), published in *Novoe Vremya*, No. 3758, 1886.

In the manifold richness of his art in relation to all social classes, Chekhov studied carefully the world of physicians and teachers, considering their role of primary importance. It is only natural that he should have been interested in medical men, who indeed almost always represented an idealistic, self-sacrificing group. Nevertheless, the author keeps his usual objectivity and shows them to us with their sorrows, problems, kindness, and faults. Doctor Kirilov struggles in vain through many sleepless nights to save his only son, watches him die, and yet in the depth of his grief and despair, starts off at the first call on a fatiguing journey ("The Enemies").[89] We meet the intelligent and lonely Doctor Ragin, who, a victim of intrigues because of his personal superiority, ends his days in his own insane asylum ("Ward No. 6"). The kind Doctor Samoilenko ("The Duel") not only offers his services freely but also considers it his duty to give all his possessions to the poor. Quite different is the fat and practical Ionych ("Ionych"), more interested in money than in the patients. The overworked Doctor Astrov, who lives among peasants and dreams of beauty (*Uncle Vanya*), the indolent Dr. Chebutykin (*The Three Sisters*), unconcerned with this world — all of them are real people drawn from real life.

As for schoolmasters, Chekhov never pictured them as happy, with the exception of Yartsev ("Three Years") and the stupid Kulygin (*The Three Sisters*). They are mostly timid, downtrodden, suffering people, living in unspeakable isolation as only the heroes of Chekhov can. In "The Horse Cart," for instance, a lonely village teacher, Maria Vasilievna, spends thirteen years among

[89] "Vragi." This recalls Henri Bordeaux's *Promenades en Savoie*, a tale of a physician who leaves his dying son, whom he cannot save, for another child whose condition is still hopeful.

peasants who dislike and mistrust her. Poor and dejected, she cries from bitter realization that life is gone without love and happiness.[90]

A profound knowledge of every aspect of life enabled Chekhov to bring into literature a wide range of portraits. All are average, unheroic people whom we may see every day, restless, unable to resist or fight, preferring abstract questions to action. With their apprehensions and tears, they bear a strong impress of femininity, typical of the prewar intelligentsia.

And above all these undecided, unhappy women and men soars the gigantic figure in "The Bishop" (1901),[91] who has no regrets, no sorrow, only a deep and profound faith. The Bishop has learned long ago that "there is no happiness, and there should not be."[92]

This statement sounds like Goethe's *"entbehren sollst Du, sollst entbehren"* (thou shalt do without).[93] But there is life and the moral law supreme for all of us — "do good." When the Bishop reads the Gospel on the Passion of Christ on Holy Thursday, he does not feel contrition. There is divine peace in his gentle soul, which at the same time is penetrated with pity for Christ, for mankind, and for himself, and tears roll down his emaciated cheeks. The same night the Bishop is taken ill and dies as quietly as a child falls asleep. "How wonderful," are his last words, "how wonderful."

Chekhov himself, searching for "faith" to replace his agnosticism or absorbed in profound meditations, often walked alone in the abandoned Moslem cemetery behind

[90] Tolstoy (*Dnievnik*, I, 115) wrote: "Have just read Chekhov's 'Na Podvode' (The Horse Cart), marvelously depicted but rhetorical."

[91] " 'Arkhiierey' is a story on a theme which has haunted me for fifteen long years," Chekhov wrote to Olga Knipper, March 16, 1901.

[92] "The Gooseberries."

[93] Goethe, *Faust*, Erster Teil, Studierzimmer. Faust says these words to Mephistopheles.

his house. His thoughts did not dwell on the past glory of Islam. Moscow alone was the center of his dreams, Moscow and Mother Russia. Disconnected visions coursed through his saddened mind. It was as if his crepuscular soul, born in the realm of shadows and premonitions, had foreseen the storms which were to fall on his native land.

In Yalta he composed his best works, in which he embodied his longings and despair. His writing of this period is saturated with deep melancholy. From the observation of triviality he more and more moved to the creation of *mood* — a strange intermixture of symbols and sounds, the accent and cadence of which were quite as important as the plot. The rattle of the watchman, the faint music of a departing regiment, and finally a sad and mysterious note coming "as if from the sky" produced a great tension in his static dramas, revealing "under apparent inertia a complex hidden action."

The everyday tragedy in *The Sea Gull*, the paralysis of soul depicted in *Uncle Vanya*, the desperate fear of life in *The Three Sisters* culminated in the last echo of a disappearing age, *The Cherry Garden* — which remained in the Russian theatre as a precious *memento mori*.

BOOK III

The Road to the Cherry Garden

XI

The Rise of the Moscow Art Theatre

WHILE Chekhov was pondering in the Crimea the awe-inspiring equation of life and death, his gaze wandering indifferently over the beautiful southern landscape, many changes in the political and literary world were in preparation. With the coming new century, an expansive influence was felt like a fresh wind. A cheerful note resounded, stronger than ever before. After the reactionary reign of Alexander III, the advent of the young Emperor Nicholas II (1894) filled all hearts with hope for a better future.

The Russians, tired of "directions" and "tendencies," were wearying of their infatuation with populism. A new era was dawning. Under the growing ascendancy of Nietzsche and Vladimir Soloviev, timid attempts were being made to find new avenues to real art and beauty. The intelligentsia even in the gloomiest days looked up to literature, which had to answer their "questions" and teach them how to live. As for the stage, they always considered it a microcosm, "a concentration and an explanation of life."[1] Therefore one of the most brilliant and important pages of Russian culture began in the history of the theatre, which began to develop later than in Western

[1] Sayler, p. 8.

Europe but progressed with such intensity that in a short time it became preëminent.

At the end of the nineteenth century the Russian stage naturally reflected the general stagnation of the epoch. This fact, already obvious to Chekhov in 1888 when he wrote his *Ivanov*, was now fully realized by the vast majority of the public. The actors were excellent.[2] The plays were, however, so poor that they hampered artistic interpretation. The realistic comedies of Ostrovsky, which dealt only with the definite milieu of the merchant classes, and translations of Scribe and Sardou comprised the usual repertoire. The theatre was maintained by a state subsidy, hence was under the management of the army of civil employees which has always overrun Russia. As they were too reactionary to lift themselves from the old rut, the stage lapsed into a condition of pitiful degeneracy until the state of affairs became unendurable.

At this time there lived in Moscow a young man upon whom fate had bestowed many gifts. Intelligent and versatile, every feature of his remarkable face expressing strength and will, tall and athletic, able to withstand any hardship, Constantine Sergeevich Alexeyev was a born leader. The son of a wealthy Moscow businessman, he had no need to choose a career and was able to devote himself to the theatre, which he passionately loved. Dissatisfied with the official stage like so many others, he turned towards the amateur drama to pursue his artistic bent. He was only twenty-two years old when, in 1885, Moscow welcomed the theatrical company of George II, Duke of Sachsen-Meiningen, which was to reveal to the world not only good playing but the real value of a per-

[2] It would be sufficient to recall a few names of many famous actors of that time at the Korsh and at the Imperial Theatres like Yermolova, Sadovskaya, Fedotova, Savina, Uzhin, Lensky, Varlamov, Davydov.

fect ensemble and of a deep psychological penetration in every individual performance.[3] All the acting of this company was a protest against the routine, the theatricality, the unnecessary declamatory pathos, which were prevailing defects of those days. In fact, the Meininger had only a few outstanding men, like the remarkable Ludwig Barnay and Josef Kainz, but the beauty of the harmonious equilibrium between the actors was quite new and produced a great effect under the leadership of the gifted stage director, Ludwig Chronegk, whom Alexeyev mentioned years later in his famous book, *My Life in Art*. The slogan of the Meininger was: *"Im Ganzen da sitzt die Macht"* (The real power is in the ensemble). Therefore, their mob scenes were particularly excellent; in Schiller's *Die Räuber* (The Brigands), for instance, there was no parading of dumb and silent performers, but a vibrating crowd of real people.

The impression made by those accomplished artistic productions was tremendous. Young Alexeyev was in ecstasy. The new theatrical company exemplified his own conception of art and stimulated him to put his own ideas into practice. In 1888 he succeeded in founding a "Society of Art and Literature," a group of amateurs who gave plays in accordance with the principles of the Meininger. In order to spare his religious and old-fashioned family, Constantine Sergeevich began to call himself Stanislavsky, a name known now to the four corners of the globe, dear not only to Russians but to all those who love the noble art of the drama.

The work of Constantine Stanislavsky, in its turn, paved the way for a more general recognition and a new understanding of the theatre. When, in 1890, the Meininger returned, they were received with great enthusiasm.

[3] Grube, p. 59.

Some playgoers, however, steeped in old traditions, ridiculed *Meiningerei* as a disease which had attacked the Russian public. In fact, this disease was spreading like a fire over all Europe. In Paris a group of amateurs opened a *Théâtre Libre* on March 30, 1887, headed by Antoine, a self-educated, gifted boy who was greatly influenced by men like Zola and Becque, who were fighting the conventionalities of the stage. Antoine, an innovator, introduced foreign playwrights: Tolstoy, Turgenev, Strindberg, and Björnson. At the same time he presented the plays of men such as Georges de Porto-Riche, Eugène Brieux, and François de Curel. His little theatre, always well attended, soon began to enjoy an international reputation and from 1897 was called *Théâtre Antoine*. In Germany there appeared the short-lived *Freie Bühne*, also a revolt against artificiality. These theatres were influencing each other, inspired from the start by the Meininger, whose principles — a perfect ensemble which excludes stardom and favoritism — they faithfully kept.

Over all this artistic ferment there loomed, like God above chaos, the gigantic shadow of Richard Wagner, who was supreme in his knowledge of the requirements of the stage. Not only was he one of the greatest composers but he was also a great writer. In the libretti written by himself, he showed to the world the unity between text and music. As early as 1876 he opened in Bayreuth his Festival Playhouse, where he succeeded in creating in his exquisite operas a perfect harmony of singing and acting against the background of an appropriate setting. Thus Richard Wagner really influenced all dramatic art in Europe by detaching it from hampering theatricality and raising the standards of good taste.

Constantine Stanislavsky, impressed by the new tendencies, conceived of "the realism of the spirit which does not depend primarily upon externals, but which is based on a sincere desire to realize and communicate to the audience the inner realities of the play."[4] Later he was to create his famous "System," which freed the actors from the banality of artificial gestures and bearing and revealed to them the simplicity of artistic perfection. These ideas he shared with Appia and with Gordon Craig, the gifted son of Ellen Terry who was introduced to Stanislavsky by Isadora Duncan and visited him in Moscow in 1911.

For twelve long years Stanislavsky dreamed of the creation of a real theatre based on new principles, but he had no one in whom to confide his thoughts until the summer of 1897, when he met another brilliant man, Vladimir Ivanovich Nemirovich-Danchenko, who taught dramatics in the Philharmonic Society and welcomed every possible chance for reform.

One day they met. Their discussion pertaining to the stage lasted no less than eighteen hours (they met at two o'clock on the afternoon of June 22 and finished at eight o'clock on the morning of June 23). Fortunately they survived, and in that long conversation they decided the fate of what was soon to be the Moscow Art Theatre, destined to play such a tremendous role in the history of Russian civilization and to become "in some ways the most illustrious of all"[5] in the realm of dramatic art.

Upon hearing of the formation of the new theatrical group the kind and sympathetic Russian press proved to be once more very encouraging: "Is it not an idle undertaking of two simpletons, a whim of the rich merchant Alexeyev and a frenzy of the writer Nemirovich?"[6] The

[4] Hughes, p. 266. [5] Hughes, p. 263.
[6] Vyshnevsky, "Kak nachinalsia Moskovskii Khudozhestvenny Teatr" (How the Moscow Art Theatre Began), in *Novy Put'*, Oct., 1928.

two simpletons, however, bravely disregarded these friendly remarks and succeeded in gathering around them educated young actors, the followers of Stanislavsky and the students of Nemirovich from the Philharmonic Society. The whole summer of 1898, unable to rent a theatre, they rehearsed in a barn at the village of Pushkino near Moscow. One could see there future stars of world renown washing floors or preparing food, so great was their enthusiasm.

The aim of Stanislavsky was "to perfect the illusion in such a way as to make it more and more representative of life." Realism, therefore, was fundamental in his representation, but he believed from the start that "realism which merely copies external aspects does not represent life. There is a hidden, inner psychological realism . . . which is elusive and extremely difficult to attain, but which goes farther than the most faithful reproduction of exterior aspects toward achieving the illusion and the interpretation of life. The aim of the Art Theatre, therefore, has been to produce the mood of a given play . . . more accurately than ever before."[7] Every emotion expressed on the stage had to be psychologically justified. Complete and perfect unity was to be reached by subordinating individual acting to the will of the stage director, who was to make it conform to the general idea of the play.

Under the combined efforts of Stanislavsky and Nemirovich the new company soon achieved that perfect ensemble they were striving for, and rented for the coming season the Hermitage Theatre in Karetny Row, which was to become famous in the annals of the Russian stage. On Wednesday, October 14, 1898, the inhabitants of Moscow read posters announcing that *"Tsar Fedor Ioannovich* — a tragedy by Count Alexey Tolstoy — would be

[7] Sayler, pp. 248-49.

presented. Tickets from 25 kopeks to eleven rubles." This spectacle aroused immediate interest, since the famous trilogy of Tolstoy (*The Death of Ioann the Terrible, Tsar Fedor,* and *Tsar Boris*) had been for thirty years banned by the censorship.

Great anxiety was felt by the new company. Before the opening they wanted a *Te Deum* sung, but this was not permitted,[8] for the theatre was considered pagan. Actors were not supposed to address their Creator on an equal footing with other good Christians. It seemed, however, that in spite of this interdiction all heavenly blessings were showered on them. Their success was immediate and overwhelming. All Moscow, confirming its reputation of being "artistic and intellectual," went to the first performance of *Tsar Fedor Ioannovich*. The public was enchanted with the new form of dramatic art. This admiration grew steadily. It has never faded, even in the subsequent tragic years of starvation, misery, and bloodshed.

Indeed, a new era began for the Russian stage. Following the impulse of the Meininger, Nemirovich and Stanislavsky, not overlooking even the smallest details, became real innovators in the search for a new atmosphere in their theatre. Instead of the irritating bell at the beginning of each act they introduced the gong. Curtains were separated instead of being raised. Lights were subdued to give the effect of cozy and relaxing mellowness.

Naturally, the greatest concern of the directors was the repertoire which should convey to the audience the new conception of art. They introduced the symbolic plays of Maeterlinck and Hauptmann. It is interesting to note that Maeterlinck's famous *The Blue Bird* (season of 1908-1909)

[8] Sobolev, *Moskovskii Khudozhestvenny Teatr* (Moscow Art Theatre), p. 22.

was given in the Art Theatre for the first time, three years before the Paris production. Stanislavsky personally met Maeterlinck and had long talks with him on art, as he himself relates in his memoirs. This meeting was preceded by an amusing incident. One of the greatest charms of Stanislavsky was his unassuming simplicity. He never realized what a great man he was. So, when invited by Maeterlinck to his château, he became quite nervous at the idea of meeting the famous writer. He wished to deliver some words of greeting and, afraid of forgetting these in his excitement, wrote them on his cuff. At the station he was met by a chauffeur and took the seat next to him. The chauffeur drove like mad while Stanislavsky memorized his greetings. Finally they arrived without a word having been spoken between them. The chauffeur, on helping him out, said, "I shall be with you in a moment." "Where is your master?" asked the surprised Stanislavsky. "I am Maeterlinck," replied the chauffeur, grinning.

The absence of the star system especially suited Chekhov's plays, of which the heroes were not heroes at all, but men and women living with the other characters on terms of touching equality. Nemirovich, a great admirer of Anton Pavlovich, asked for permission to produce *The Sea Gull*, "this marvelous representation of the human soul."[9] Chekhov had an appeal for the actors of the young Theatre as an interpreter of a new form of art built on a profound knowledge of human psychology, the delicate nuances of which were expressed in odd dialogue, in a general slowing down of the speech, in subdued voices, and finally in the creation of that elusive atmosphere which

[9] Nemirovich-Danchenko to Chekhov, April 25, 1898. Nemirovich so greatly admired Chekhov that he refused the "Griboedov Prize" for his own play *Tsena Zhizni* (Price of Life), 1896, despite its great success, because he believed that it belonged to the author of *The Sea Gull*.

from that time on received the name of *mood* (*nastroenie*). His dramas gave Stanislavsky a stimulating opportunity to put in practice the theories of the Art Theatre as stated by Nemirovich: "To give back to the stage a living psychology and simple speech. To examine life not only through rising heights and falling abysses but through the every-day life surrounding us. . . . The art of Tchekhov is the art of artistic freedom and artistic truth."[10]

Chekhov, on receiving the request of Nemirovich, at first refused. Painful memories were too fresh in his mind; he was terrified at the mere thought of witnessing a second failure. But urged from all sides, never able to resist, he finally consented.

The Art Theatre began to rehearse *The Sea Gull* with great care and equally great apprehension. Chekhov came to the rehearsals, but was not always satisfied. He believed that in many productions of the new Theatre the ultra-realistic effects were considerably overstressed. Vsevolod Meyerhold, one of the leading actors, remembers that when Anton Pavlovich was told that in his play the grasshoppers would chirr, the frogs croak, the dragonflies buzz, and the dogs bark, he could not suppress a feeling of disappointment.

"What is that for?" he asked, not without asperity.

"Because it is true to nature."

"True to nature," said Anton Pavlovich, laughing. "Kramsky, a genre painter, has a picture where faces are beautifully painted. What would it be if we would cut out the nose of one of these faces, and put in a real one? The nose is 'real' but the picture has been ruined." And he added, "The stage requires a certain conventionality, the fourth wall is lacking there. Besides, the stage is an art.

[10] Quoted in Sayler, p. 249.

It reflects the quintessence of life and should avoid any redundant details."[11]

The directors themselves realized that the *mood* of Chekhov is "often beyond the reach of mere consciousness." They tried to create an autumnal atmosphere in the *mise en scène* of *The Sea Gull* where the faint lights of the evening were succeeded by the pale beams of the moon rising over a lonely, silver-brown world.

The circumstances which preceded this performance were depressing. Chekhov was almost carried off by a dreadful hemorrhage. His sister, much alarmed, begged the directors to drop the performance, so great was her anxiety over a possible second failure, which might kill Anton Pavlovich. But to give up the play would have meant ruin for the new company. So all the actors decided: "We must play, we must create not only success, but triumph." One has only to read Stanislavsky's *My Life in Art* to grasp the magnitude of this event. December 16, 1898, when *The Sea Gull* was presented, was certainly *the* date in the life of the young theatre. The evening began in an atmosphere of terrific nervous tension. Constantine Stanislavsky, experiencing an unusual excitement, walked up and down speaking encouraging words to his hysterical colleagues. Then, to reassure himself, he started a wild dance, known in the annals of the theatre as the "dance of death." But soon the gong was heard and the terrified actors went to the stage as one approaches the scaffold. Stanislavsky tells us: "How we played, I do not remember. The first act terminated in the complete silence of the audience. One actress fainted. I could hardly stand on my feet from despair. Then suddenly, after a long pause, there was heard a noise, a roar, and then mad applause. The curtains began to separate, came back together, and we stood dumb

[11] Meyerhold, p. 24.

We stood motionless, not realizing that we had to bow. At last we felt that we were successful, and, unspeakably stirred, embraced each other, as on Easter Night."[12]

So, under the masterful direction of the highly gifted Nemirovich and of Stanislavsky, with educated, intelligent actors, *The Sea Gull* had a success that surpassed the most optimistic expectations. Moscow was completely under its spell, and looked down at chilly St. Petersburg, the young *parvenu* that had shown such bad taste in not recognizing a masterpiece. Of course one could hear: "We in Moscow certainly knew better."

Stanislavsky, who played Trigorin, was splendidly supported by the whole cast. Even the minor roles of Medvedenko and Shamraev were performed by accomplished actors. Every member of the company was a star, confirming "the most fundamental, the most universal theory in Russia, that the theatre is an art, and everyone connected with it must be an artist." That is why "the Russian theatre has attained the leadership of the world."[13]

Tickets were sold out for all performances of *The Sea Gull*. The public, tense and receptive, concentrated its attention on every word of the play. Full houses and an enthusiastic reception stimulated the actors to do still better work. At times it seemed as if a segment of real life were shown on the stage. Prince Urusov wrote in admiration to Chekhov: "Moscow is literally in love with your play; the universal question now is 'Have you seen *The Sea Gull*?' They will be writing about it long after we are gone."[14]

Chekhov, whose condition was most precarious, could not believe at first in his great success. He thought he was being deceived because of his illness. When he was at last convinced, he wrote in ecstasy to Vyshnevsky, an actor in

[12] Stanislavsky, p. 298.   [13] Sayler, p. 261.
[14] Prince Urusov to Chekhov, Jan. 5, 1899.

the Moscow Art Theatre: "I send you a great big six-story thanks for your nice telegram, which I shall keep as a souvenir. Sometime, in about twenty years, I will show it to you. In the beginning I couldn't understand a thing in the newspapers. Then my brother Ivan came to Yalta, a letter arrived from Vladimir Ivanovich [Nemirovich], and I realized how well you played, how good it was altogether, and how absurd that I had not been in Moscow. When shall I see *The Sea Gull*?"[15]

Had Chekhov not been living in Yalta, this winter would have been the happiest in his life. Even his health improved slightly under the beneficial influence of unexpected good fortune. In March he was able to go to Moscow and to see a performance of *The Sea Gull*, which he described as "brilliant."

The enthusiastic reception of his play proved to Chekhov that there were great possibilities for his dramatic aspirations in pursuit of "inward and outward artistic truth," which served as a foundation for the "Stanislavsky System." Stanislavsky and his colleagues therefore began to call their theatre "The Chekhov Theatre," definitely accepting him as their playwright and *The Sea Gull* — their mutual success — as their emblem.

A profound understanding united Chekhov with the new company, the members of which appreciated his literary work so highly that Moskvin, one of the greatest comedians of the Russian stage, became the acknowledged reader of his humorous stories. New plays were expected from him. Anton Pavlovich at last felt encouraged. He rewrote his unsuccessful *The Wood Spirit*, which had been performed in the provinces under the title of *Uncle Vanya*. The comments on it were relatively favorable, and Chekhov consented to give it to the Art Theatre, as recorded by

[15] Chekhov to Vyshnevsky, Dec. 26, 1898.

Constantine Stanislavsky: "The play was given to us. We started immediately to work on it, taking advantage of Anton Pavlovich's presence in order to conform to his wishes."[16]

Uncle Vanya illustrates the development and the increasing depth of Chekhov's talent. Like *Ivanov* it is entirely static, but one discerns a new element in it — the absence of a definite end. As in his tales, the playwright takes only a "slice of life" and leaves it to the audience to imagine what has preceded it and what will follow. The protagonists tell about their lives only what is necessary for the understanding of their roles in the play. As usual, they are unheroic; life has blunted their feelings: "I don't need a thing, I like nobody" (Doctor Astrov, Act I). Nothing happens in the gray monotony of their existence; therefore the plot is unimportant — one might say absent. Here are simply "scenes from country life in four acts."

Professor Serebriakov, who for twenty-five years has lectured and written about art, feels that he missed his life in "ruminating over other people's thoughts." Now, old and worn out, he ardently "wants to live," like Sorin in *The Sea Gull.* He returns for peace and rest to the estate of his daughter Sonya, who manages it with Uncle Vanya, her mother's brother. The latter has lived for twenty-five years in complete admiration of his brother-in-law, but, on seeing him at close quarters, realizes that he has "wasted his time, when he might have been winning everything that age now forbids." His hatred is intensified by the love he feels for the professor's second wife, the charming Helena Andreevna, a "siren," depicted as one of those idle women who bring nothing but disturbance into the peaceful lives of men. She is very unhappy with her old husband, whom she had married in the belief that he was a great man.

[16] Stanislavsky, p. 301.

His mediocrity and selfishness repel her, and, if she does not betray him, it is only because of the "morality of her indolence." In her solitude she could have fallen in love with Doctor Astrov, who comes to treat her "gout-ridden" professor, but she is a coward, afraid that her "conscience may torment her." Doctor Astrov indeed is "handsome, interesting and charming." He is "different" from everybody else. Though he has been somewhat coarsened by daily contact with peasants, he appreciates and loves nature and longs for refinement and beauty, which alone "have the power to touch him still." He thinks that in a human being everything should be beautiful — face, soul, attire, thought — especially since the routine of Russian life is "prosaic and has no redeeming features." And Astrov, the "thinking realist," believes in work, believes that an "idle existence can never be a pure one." A country doctor, on his feet "from dawn to dusk," his thoughts dwell always on his profession. He cannot forget that "during Lent one of his patients died under chloroform," thus displaying like Ivanov that purely Russian trait — the obsession of guilt which makes him self-conscious and "numbs his feelings." He is no longer capable of love, though he is attracted to Helena, who brings with her the beauty he has always longed for. As in *The Sea Gull*, there are many conversations and odd bits of dialogue, giving the impression that the heroes follow their own thoughts without trying to be intelligible to others. The action is developed casually until the professor precipitates the conflict. Bored with the country, he wishes to sell the estate, which belongs partly to his daughter and partly to Uncle Vanya, who generously gave his share to his late sister when she married Serebriakov. That decision infuriates Vanya. It would deprive him of his last abode, and he realizes that he has stupidly ruined his life in sacrificing it to his ungrateful brother-in-law. Like all the heroes of Chekhov, he craves appreciation and recognition. Treplev in *The Sea Gull* claimed that he was more "talented" than the others. So does Uncle Vanya: "I am intelligent, brave, and strong. If I had lived normally, I might have become another Schopenhauer . . . or Dostoyevsky." This dissatisfied country gentleman is one of the most touching figures in the gallery of Chekhov's portraits.[17] In elegance and beauty he seeks oblivion from the drabness of his life. There is an infinite sadness in his bringing Helena "autumnal roses, beautiful, sad roses" to create an illusion of happiness where real "life is wanting." Rejected by the woman he deeply loves, unappreciated by the old professor, Uncle Vanya in despair shoots at his brother-in-law but misses. His rebellion is short-lived. The fight is aimless, he knows it, and loses his courage, while Doctor Astrov, who has no longer the faculty of being compassionate, indifferently says: "You and I have but one hope, that we may be visited by visions, perhaps by pleasant ones, as we lie resting in our graves." Astrov, too, believes that Helena and the old professor infect people with their laziness and carry destruction with them. Therefore, when Vanya weeps at her departure, he only whistles as he gazes at the map of distant Africa. "It must be boiling hot over there . . . dreadful." (Because of these words Maxim Gorky claimed that Chekhov was colder towards mankind than the devil himself.) Constantine Stanislavsky, who created an unforgettable portrait of Doctor Astrov, remembers that it was the author himself who insisted that he should whistle during the last scene, in order to show his fatigue and indifference. Yet, at the end, something

---

[17] When the actor Vyshnevsky, who played Uncle Vanya, neglected his appearance, Chekhov protested: "Our landowners are wonderful, cultured people, they dress well." Stanislavsky, pp. 301-3.

moves Astrov's tired soul strangely: "How odd we meet, and then must part forever."

Sonya, the sweet but unattractive stepdaughter of Helena, in love with Astrov, who does not even notice her, still keeps, despite her personal grief, her childlike faith and tries to console Uncle Vanya. "We must live our lives. Yes, we shall live, Uncle Vanya. We shall live through the long procession of days before us; we shall patiently bear the trials that fate imposes on us . . . We shall work for others without rest . . . and when our last hour comes, we shall meet it humbly, and there, beyond the grave, we shall say that we have suffered and wept, that our life was bitter, and God will have pity on us. Ah, then, dear, dear Uncle, we shall see that bright and beautiful life . . . We shall rest. We shall hear the angels. We shall see heaven shining like jewels . . . I have faith. I have faith . . ."

Only Marina, the tired old nurse, remains unperturbed among all these distressed people. She is very happy that the Serebriakovs are gone: "Now everything will be as it was before. We shall have order as decent people, as Christians like to have it." And she adds with a sigh: "It is long since I have eaten noodles." Mingled with all those dreams of noodles and of heaven shining like diamonds, the watchman's rattle is heard as the reminder of fleeting time, of hours forever lost in the past.

This drama of depression and hopelessness is built more on details than on plot. The desolation of the characters, that beloved and ever-repeated theme, is combined with a strange tension, completely out of proportion to the triviality of the life depicted. It would have been violently attacked again had it not been for the actors of the Moscow Art Theatre, who understood the sorrowful lyricism of Chekhov. In their masterful interpretation, *Uncle Vanya* met with a great success. Maxim Gorky, who was the man of the decade, voiced the general impression when he wrote to Chekhov on December 18, 1899: "Have seen *Uncle Vanya* recently; while seeing it, wept like an old woman, although I am far from being sentimental; returned home stunned . . . by your play. . . . Watching its heroes, I felt as if I were sawed by a blunt saw. We are unhappy, tedious people — that is true. It seems to me that in this play you are colder towards mankind than the devil himself. . . . Maupassant is excellent; I like him very much . . . you I like better."

The *unity of mood* that replaced the unity of action was generally acclaimed. The same *Homo Novus* (A. Kugel) who spoke of Chekhov's morbidity in *The Sea Gull*, stated that *Uncle Vanya* was one of the most interesting performances he had seen in a long while.

It seemed that Tolstoy alone disapproved of the play, calling its heroes trashy. In his diary, January 27, 1900, he wrote: "Went to see *Uncle Vanya* and became indignant." Vyshnevsky, who played Uncle Vanya, remembered that Tolstoy said to him: "Why do you pester another man's wife? Can't you get a farm girl for yourself?"[18] And to Chekhov Tolstoy repeated time and again: "You are good, Anton Pavlovich, but your plays are bad all the same," and he, who "disliked Elizabethan exuberance"[19] like Voltaire, continued: "I cannot bear Shakespeare, you know, but your plays are even worse. Shakespeare, for all that, takes the reader by the neck and leads him to a certain goal, and does not let him turn aside. And where is one to go with your heroes? From the sofa where they are lying to the closet and back!"[20]

Despite this severe criticism from the "Great Old Man,"

[18] Vyshnevsky, "Kak nachinalsia Moskovskii Khudozhestvenny Teatr" (How the Moscow Art Theatre Began), in *Novy Put'* October, 1928.

[19] Mirsky, *Contemporary Russian Literature,* p. 16.

[20] Chekhov, Appendix, Gosisdat edition of complete works.

Uncle Vanya was received with much applause because with its prevailing gloom it still reflected the mood of the vast majority. As in the '40s, when Hegel, Fichte, and Schlegel were the only gods worthy of adoration, the Russian society of the '80s and the '90s had fallen into a trance before another divinity, Arthur Schopenhauer, who seemed to answer all their needs. The ardor with which the Russians accepted every new idea from outside had already been noted by Dostoyevsky in his *Author's Diary* (1873). Now the followers of the German philosopher became so numerous that they provoked shouts of indignation on the part of the old-fashioned religious people, who, in order to combat his influence, attacked *Novoe Vremya* for having printed articles on Arthur Schopenhauer. Suvorin on March 29, 1897 entered in his diary some excerpts from these attacks, which he also reprinted from various papers in his daily: "The world outlook of the moralists of *Novoe Vremya* is very similar to the false teachings of the atheist Schopenhauer and his incorrigible follower, L. Tolstoy. Schopenhauer calls the basic principle not God but Will. . . . The teaching of that dreamer, whose psychic abnormality is obvious, finds a systematic apology in Suvorin's daily. They repeat that Schopenhauer is the 'genius of the century, the true master of our epoch.' Our epoch, full of all kinds of grief, is extremely favorable to Schopenhauer. He is a modern thinker. Youth swears by him, believing him to bring truth to life, and wishes nothing else but him."[21] "For many, the theories of Schopenhauer became a sort of gospel."[22] The influence of the German philosopher, who inspired Wagner, Nietzsche, and Renan, was indeed tremendous. Tolstoy called him "the greatest among men."[23] Chekhov also, as a son of his generation,

[21] Suvorin's diary for March 29, 1897.
[22] *Novoe Vremya*, No. 5553.
[23] Letter to the poet Fet, Aug. 30, 1869.

was attracted by pessimism, which is revealed in his story, "The Lights" (1888). He read Arthur Schopenhauer, whose works were to be found in Chekhov's library in Yalta. However, he always kept his freedom of unprejudiced thought. Alexey Suvorin, in his obituary of July 4, 1904, and Maxim Kovalevsky, in the memoirs mentioned above, have both stated, knowing him intimately, that Chekhov never adhered to any definite philosophical system. So, when he put into the mouth of his heroes in *Uncle Vanya* and *The Wood Spirit* (variations of the same theme printed nine years apart) the words: "If I had lived normally, I might have become another Schopenhauer . . . or Dostoyevsky," he simply acknowledged the great ascendancy of those men, just as he acknowledged the influence of Ibsen, also much admired by his generation. When Uncle Vanya and Treplev awake for a moment from their habitual lethargy, they not only seek recognition, but they insist on their human rights, remembering that everyone has duties towards himself first of all, a thought already expressed by Nora in *A Doll's House* in 1879. The greatest merit of Chekhov, a true representative of his epoch, lies precisely in the fact that, being extremely sensitive, he reflected in his works all the tendencies and currents of that yesterday which seems to be separated from our own day by centuries. And what appears even more important is the fact that he knew, better than any other Russian writer, how to depict, not the "rising heights" of life, but its everyday occurrences, and to show us the banality of human existence with a mastery which has not been surpassed.

Uncle Vanya was given for the first time on October 26, 1899 in the absence of Chekhov, who was living, as usual, at Yalta. The Moscow Art Theatre kept him informed by wire about the performance. "The telegrams began to arrive the 27th in the evening, when I was in bed. They were transmitted to me by telephone. I woke up and went barefoot to receive the message. No sooner had I gone back to sleep than the bell rang again and again. For the first time my own glory prevented me from sleeping."[24] And Chekhov conceived the idea of inviting the "glorious theatre" to visit him at Yalta: "I have a request," he wrote to Vyshnevsky. "Ask Vladimir Ivanovich [Nemirovich] and Constantine Sergeevich [Stanislavsky] to come south to play, and at the same time have some rest."[25]

At Easter the whole Moscow Art Theatre went to the Crimea to console and cheer Anton Pavlovich. Stanislavsky describes in his book[26] how "actors, their wives, children, nurses, property-men, costumers, hairdressers, several cars with luggage, set out in the worst spring weather from chilly Moscow towards the southern sun, to white Sebastopol. . . . We have shown *Uncle Vanya* to Chekhov . . . it was a tremendous success. . . . This time he was satisfied with the performance. In the intermission he came to me and lauded us. At the end he made only one remark: 'He whistles, listen to me, he whistles.'" Chekhov meant Doctor Astrov.

"From Sebastopol," Stanislavsky further relates, "we went to Yalta, where almost the whole Russian literary world was expecting us — Bunin, Kuprin, Mamin-Siberiak, Chirikov, Stanukovich, Elpatievsky and finally Maxim Gorky, whose popularity had begun to grow." It was there that Gorky mentioned for the first time his famous play *In the Depths*, which two years later was produced by the Art Theatre. Chekhov later wrote to him in great appreciation: "I have read your play; it is unmistakably fine.

[24] Chekhov to Olga Knipper, Oct. 30, 1899.
[25] Chekhov to Vyshnevsky, Nov. 3, 1899.
[26] Stanislavsky, p. 304.

The second act is very good. It is the best and the strong-
est. . . . Vyshnevsky walks about the house and imagines
himself The Tartar [a character in the play]. The part of
The Actor, in which you have been very successful, will
be given to an experienced man — perhaps Stanislavsky
himself. Kachalov will take the role of The Baron."[27]
Chekhov was right in his prognosis. The play aroused
general enthusiasm.

Meanwhile, the success of *Uncle Vanya* and *The Sea
Gull* in the Crimea was tremendous. The sublime tech-
nique of the actors, combined with their thoroughness and
intelligence, revealed to everyone, especially to Chekhov
himself, that he was truly a dramatist. He considered it
the culmination of his happiness to have met the Art Theatre, which he called a "beautiful oasis in the sea of banality."[28] The two weeks the new company spent in Yalta
were like an exquisite dream for Anton Pavlovich, in whose
house they gathered for luncheon every day. He kept in
his garden as some of his most precious possessions the
swing and the bench from the play *Uncle Vanya*, which
reminded him of the visit of his new friends. After their
departure, he experienced again the acute sensation of
loneliness. Only work helped him to forget his involuntary
exile. Seated in his shady garden he wrote the whole morning until noon, when "his house filled with visitors. . . .
Various people came to call on Chekhov: scholars, writers,
district councilors, medical men, army officers, painters, admirers of both sexes, professors, society people, senators,
priests, actors, and heavens knows who else. . . . Despite
the fatigue of this merry-go-round, there was something in
it that appealed to Chekhov; he learned everything that
happened in Russia at first hand. Not all the guests spared

[27] Chekhov to Maxim Gorky, July 29, 1902.
[28] Chekhov to Vyshnevsky, Nov. 3, 1899.

the time and the nerves of Anton Pavlovich. Some of them were merciless."[29] N. S. Butova, an actress of the Moscow Art Theatre, remembers, that he once showed her his field glasses, and called them laughingly his only salvation.

" 'How is that?' asked Madame Butova.

" 'Well, when the visitors come and begin to philosophize, I take the field glasses and look, during the day at the sea, at night at the sky. Guests imagine that I am thinking about something deep and stop their discourse for fear of disturbing me.' . . . Soon a lady came in. . . . She started at once to talk about his writing. For a long time Chekhov remained silent. Finally he requested: 'Masha [his sister], bring me my field glasses.' "[30]

The fair sex, indeed, became sometimes unbearable. Gorky remembers that "three luxuriously dressed ladies came to see him; they filled the room with the rustle of silk skirts and the smell of strong perfume; they sat down politely opposite their host, pretended that they were interested in politics, and began 'putting questions' about the war between the Turks and Greeks: 'and whom do you like best?' Anton Pavlovich looked up kindly and answered with a meek smile: 'I love candied fruits . . . don't you?' " Another time, "a plump, handsome, well-dressed lady came to him and began to speak à la Chekhov: 'Life is so boring, Anton Pavlovich, everything is so gray — people, the sea, even the flowers seem to me gray . . . and I have no desires . . . my soul is in pain . . . it is like a disease' . . . 'It is a disease,' said Anton Pavlovich with conviction. 'It is a disease; in Latin it is called *morbus fraudulentus.*' "

"A Russian is a strange creature," Chekhov said once. "in order to live well and humanly one must work — work

---

[29] Kuprin's recollections, in *Chekhovskii sbornik*, pp. 95-109.
[30] Feider, p. 357.

with love and with faith. But we cannot do it." And Gorky concludes: "Anton Pavlovich in his early stories was already able to reveal, in the dim sea of banality, its tragic humor; one has only to read his *humorous* stories with attention to see what a lot of cruel and disgusting things, behind the humorous words and situations, had been observed with sorrow by the author. . . . In each of his humorous stories I hear the quiet, deep sigh of a pure human heart, the hopeless sigh of sympathy for men who do not know how to respect human dignity, who submit without any resistance to mere force and live like fish."[31]

Chekhov was always painfully conscious of the inefficiency and weakness of the Russian character. These traits may be found even in his early tales. In his youth Antosha Chekhonte laughed in depicting the negative sides of his epoch, whereas now he experienced a deep sadness, which reached its climax in the Crimean banishment. There he wrote the gloomiest of his plays, *The Three Sisters,* which, beneath its tears, revealed amazing glimpses into the future while stigmatizing the pathetic instability of the prewar intelligentsia.

[31] Gorky, "Anton Tchekhov: Fragments of Recollections," pp. 97-105.

XII

Fulfillment

THE autumn of 1900 Chekhov decided to spend in
Moscow. Stanislavsky relates: "We nagged him all the time
to give us another play. From his letters we knew that he
was writing about military circles, but we could not guess
from his short, abrupt sentences what the plot was about.
We were begging him to send the play quickly."[32] He
lingered, however, and in his long missives complained of
being "cruelly, disgustingly, wickedly disturbed. . . . The
play is crystallized in my head, just ready to be written,
but I hardly sit down before the door opens and some
dolt comes crawling in."[33] No wonder that weeks elapsed
before he could notify his friends that his drama was at
last finished. Anton Pavlovich brought it himself, happy
at having a pretext to visit again the old city to which he
was bound by family ties, by friendship, and now by his
"autumnal" love for Olga Knipper, the gifted actress of
the Art Theatre who had decidedly interested him for
several years. Already in 1898 (October 8) he wrote to
Suvorin from Yalta: "Before my departure I attended the
rehearsals of *Tsar Fedor Ioannovich*. I was moved by the
intelligence which marked the performance. Real art was

[32] Feider, p. 362.
[33] Chekhov to Olga Knipper, Aug. 20, 1900.

on the stage. . . . Irena [Olga Knipper] I think excellent. Her voice, the elevation of her character, her sincerity are so wonderful that I enjoy the mere recollection of it. . . . Best of all is Irena! If I had stayed in Moscow I should have fallen in love with that Irena."

It was the first time that the secretive Chekhov indulged in such an extraordinary confidence. Seemingly this attachment was strong. Nothing would have pleased him better than to have remained in Moscow in the society of brilliant men like Stanislavsky and women like the charming Olga Knipper. We know he fell in love with Moscow the very day he was told in the private hospital of Professor Ostroumov that he could no longer live in the North. But since he had made contact with the Art Theatre, this city became for him what Mecca and Medina are for the worshipper of Allah and his Prophet. It was the paradise on earth, the beginning and end of everything. Chekhov's life, however, always full of restrictions and frustrations, seemed fated to be a panorama of changing environments; he was obliged once more to leave for Italy and the Riviera. In great agitation and nervousness, he handed his new play to Stanislavsky before he left.

Upon reading *The Three Sisters* the actors remained in perplexed silence. "It is not a play, but only a scheme, it cannot be played; there are no roles but only hints, intimations," they were saying. Chekhov in terrible confusion walked back and forth, smiled, and coughed.[34] What always surprised him, as Stanislavsky recollected, was that *The Three Sisters* and later *The Cherry Garden* were considered as gloomy dramas of Russian life. He was sincerely convinced that they were gay comedies, almost vaudeville.

Nevertheless, the play was accepted and the actors began to work on it with their usual thoroughness. Anton Pavlo-

[34] Feider, p. 363.

vich went abroad. From Nice he bombarded Olga Knipper with letters. "Describe to me at least one of your rehearsals! Is there anything to add or to shorten? Are you playing well? [Miss Knipper played the second of the sisters, Masha.] Beware, do not make a sad face in any act. An angry one, yes, but not sad. People who carry sorrow in themselves are used to it. They only whistle or are plunged in deep reveries. In view of that, be thoughtful on the stage while talking." "Why is there noise in the third act? Noise is only in the distance, indistinguishable and dim. On the stage itself everyone is tired, almost asleep. . . . I said that Tuzenbach's body should not be carried across your stage, but Alexeyev [Stanislavsky] insisted."[35]

Chekhov often disagreed with Stanislavsky over the pronounced emphasis on the realistic effects, which were in contradiction to his light, ethereal plays. Lovers of music will remember that upon writing his beautiful *Pastoral Symphony*,[36] Beethoven said: *"Mehr Empfindung als Malerei"* (More emotion than delineation). This slogan of the great master of symphonic art might also have been that of Chekhov, whose works were built on *leit-motifs* and had musical fluidity, that "movement of slowness and rapidity"[37] which is particularly difficult to represent and which eludes the stage and its conventions.

Chekhov loved to introduce definite sounds in order to create a definite mood intended to bring out the hidden symbols of his plays, yet he hated noise as unnecessary and harmful, likely to divide the attention of the audience instead of concentrating it on the ideas of the author. His delicacy prevented him from expressing his criticism. When he disapproved of something or was dissatisfied with the

[35] Chekhov to Olga Knipper, Jan. 2 and Jan. 28, 1901.
[36] *Pastoral Symphony*, the Sixth, in F-dur, 1808.
[37] Lessing, p. 34.

rehearsals, he used to say that he was "somewhat cold, or that he was not feeling well." Only once he said, so that Stanislavsky could hear him: "I will write a new play and it shall begin thus, 'Oh, how marvelous, how still! One does not hear either dogs or birds or cuckoos, owls, nightingales, clocks, bells, or even crickets.' " "Of course," adds Stanislavsky, "I understood that this veiled allusion was meant for me."[38]

The Three Sisters was given at the Art Theatre on January 31, 1901, again without Chekhov. Little is known about the genesis of this gloomy play. Maxim Kovalevsky tells us in the unpublished memoirs already mentioned that Chekhov, upon reading the proofs in Florence, expressed his dissatisfaction. He often complained that a great number of characters encumbered the smooth flow of dramatic development. The external episodes were reminiscent of the author's life in Voskresensk, where he was a guest of his brother Ivan in 1884. Both of them met Colonel Mayevsky frequently, and Mayevsky, under the name of Colonel Vershinin, appears in the drama.

It is clear that the three sisters embody restlessness and strain, traits typical of Chekhov at that time. Their ever-repeated outcry, "Moscow! Moscow!" —where they never go despite the fact that they are free to do whatever they please— is nothing but the wail of the author himself, whose unkind fate kept him away from that city. The play reminds one of Sinclair Lewis's *Main Street* except that it has not the American sense of practical values but is saturated with Russian lyricism and hysteria. Written like *The Sea Gull* and *Uncle Vanya*, its center of gravity lies not in the plot, but in the emotional nuances. It has the same curious, moonlike strangeness, and in its dim and hazy atmosphere you can hear the faint sound of a distant aeolian

[38] Stanislavsky, p. 360.

harp. This is a profound drama of weak, idle people who, in the monotony of a provincial existence, idealize the life outside. Therefore, they talk frantically about work, torn between the desire to do something they have never done and the realization of their own helplessness. They live in the distress of an abnormal morbid tension, never relieved by any exterior action. That point is particularly interesting. Chekhov, overworked and ill, had often emphasized the blessings of idleness: "I believe that nearness to nature and idleness form the necessary element of happiness, which is impossible without them," he wrote to Suvorin on May 9, 1894, and to Lika on March 27, 1894: "I believe that real happiness is impossible without idleness. For me the greatest delight is to walk or to sit or to do nothing. My favorite occupation is to do the unnecessary," and with a sudden awakening of the laughing Antosha Chekhonte he adds unexpectedly, "and to love a plump girl" [Lika was plump]. In his *Note-Books* he entered the observation: "Life disagrees with philosophy, there is no happiness without idleness; only the useless is pleasurable."[39] It has been generally noticed that he often depicted people who do nothing and who are superior to their environment because they live in the ideal world of dreams and contemplations.

On the other hand, Chekhov, always intricate, realized that one must work. Doctor Astrov in *Uncle Vanya* claims that an "idle existence can never be a pure one." And Irena, the most helpless of the three sisters, unfit for any exertion of will, exalts all forms of activity, even the physical, as if to counterbalance her own weakness. She says: "Whoever he may be, a man must work, for that is the meaning and object of life. . . . How fine it is to be a workman who gets up at sunrise and breaks stones in the street, or a shepherd, or a schoolmaster who teaches chil-

[39] Chekhov, *Note-Books*, p. 85.

dren, or an engine-driver on the railway. . . . Let alone a
man, it's better to be an ox, or a horse, so long as it can
work. . . . Sometimes when it's hot, your thirst can be
just as tiresome as my need for work."

Life is changing, this fact is obvious to the timid heroes
of Chekhov. Baron Tuzenbach expresses this belief in
prophetical words: "A new age is dawning, the people are
marching on us all. A powerful, health-giving storm is
gathering, it is drawing near, soon it will be upon us, and
it will drive out laziness, indifference, prejudice against
work, and rotten dullness from our society."

Despite the traditions of his family, the young lieutenant
decides to quit the army. Restless, like all Chekhovian
heroes, he is convinced that elsewhere he will be more use-
ful and happy. The middle-aged Colonel Vershinin also
believes in work, "much work." But he thinks that the
results will be noticeable only "in two or three hundred
years" and then "existence on earth will be unspeakably
beautiful and wonderful." As for the present, he sees it
with sad eyes: "We Russians are extremely gifted in thinking on an exalted plane, but why do we aim so low in life?
Why?" And he repeats the inner thought of Chekhov:
"There is no happiness for us, there should not and cannot
be. . . . We must work, while happiness is only for our
distant posterity." Colonel Vershinin deplores the fact "that
youth is gone" (another favorite *leit-motif* of the author,
expressed also in "The Peasants") ; he knows that he will
never have even a foretaste of that splendor and glory
which is in store for humanity. Yet he likes to "philosophize at any rate" — unable to find in any activity consolation for the flying years.

Only the old Doctor Chebutykin does not indulge in
daydreaming. He asks nothing more of life. Like the professor in "The Dreary Story," he has lost his illusions and

does not believe in the glorious future of mankind. His only interest is centered on the three sisters, whom he loves like his own daughters. Yet, when Baron Tuzenbach, Irena's fiancé, is killed in the duel, Doctor Chebutykin exclaims: "One baron more or less — what difference does it make? It is all the same." Indeed, what does it matter? "Perhaps we only think that we live, when in reality we don't."

At first glance the characters appear somewhat unreal. They speak unnaturally in affectedly chosen words, are easily given to tears. They are like dark shadows hardly perceptible on the dim background of the autumnal setting. But soon we begin to distinguish their contours.

Sometimes, in going through old desks, we may find there piles of forgotten letters. We turn the yellow leaves in amusement; we read and suddenly we feel that these faded pages emit a faint aroma of a distant past lost in oblivion. Dim memories become concrete and precise and slowly we begin to remember the bygone days always dear to our hearts.

So is it with the art of Chekhov. Sometime, somewhere we have known his elusive heroes; we recognize them at last. The slender Irena, dressed in white, her dark hair fluffed up according to the fashion of her time, wears most likely on a black velvet ribbon a golden medallion containing the portrait of her dead mother. Her fingers clutch a book which she does not read. She is sad, that "lonely stranger,"[40] entirely unadapted to life: "I am unhappy, unhappy! I can't work, I shan't work. Enough, enough! I have nothing but hate and contempt for all they give me to do." Her elder sister, Olga, in the blue uniform of a schoolmistress, is kind and good, but unspeakably bored with her existence. She is crushed by the law of recurrence,

[40] Andrey, a character in *The Three Sisters*, uses this expression in Act II.

which she cannot endure. Olga is deeply concerned about the future of her younger sister. Perhaps there is happiness in marriage; she advises Irena to marry Tuzenbach. Irena agrees, on the condition that they go away: "I'll marry him, I'll consent, only let's go to Moscow! I implore you, let's go. There is nothing better than Moscow on earth."

It never occurs to them that they have not seen anything else in their lives but the vague mirage of the city. Steeped in their own exaggerated suffering and useless chatter, they do not notice that Masha, the second sister and usually the most energetic of the three, has now much sorrow of her own. Masha married at eighteen the stupid Kulygin, a teacher of classical languages who impressed her with his Latin sayings and seemed at that time the epitome of wisdom. She was, however, soon disillusioned, and now she is in love with Colonel Vershinin: "I want to make a confession, dear sisters, my soul is in pain. I love, I love, I love that man." Yet she realizes that they talk the whole day through to no avail. Their brother Andrey wanted to be a professor but instead marries the repulsive Natasha, who with her "scrubbed cheeks," wearing "a queer bright . . . skirt with a wretched little fringe" is a wicked "little bourgeoise." Natasha never forgets the cool reception she got (in the first act) nor Olga's rebuke for her poor taste. After she is married she takes her revenge in becoming a tyrannical mistress of the household. Andrey feels that he is a failure. He regrets his past but does not try in any way to change his present: "Why do we, almost before we have begun to live, become dull, gray, . . . useless and unhappy?" Yet even he, who, indeed, is uninteresting and lazy, believes like all the Chekhovian heroes that the present is beastly but the future will be wonderful. "There is light in the distance, I see freedom . . . I feel so light and free." He does nothing, however, but push the baby-carriage, because he has been ordered to do so by his unscrupulous wife, under whose influence he mortgages the house of his sisters and spends all the money. Finally, when the girls are driven out of their own home, he does not protect them. He is just as vulgar as the self-satisfied, mediocre Natasha. The sisters do not defend their rights; on the contrary, they avoid all explanation with their brother and go away without protest, as does the timid and frightened Lipa in "In the Ravine." They have not the strength to fight. Life has robbed them of the last resource, their hope for possible happiness. Baron Tuzenbach is killed in a duel and the frail Irena, whose "paleness shines through darkness as if it were light," feels that fate has nothing more in store for her. Masha loves Colonel Vershinin, but he is married, his regiment is transferred, and they know that they will never see each other again. Olga, driven out of her own home, accepts definitely a paid position in her school and knows that she will never go to Moscow. Andrey is fully aware that he will never become a worthy man.

The young lieutenants, Fedotik and Rodé, come to take a snapshot of their friends "for the last time." Bidding them good-bye, they repeat the words of Doctor Astrov: "We never meet again." The three sisters present a picture of gloom as the music of the departing regiment grows fainter and fainter, and its last echo dissolves in the weird, motionless, crepuscular world. They know that they will never leave this dull town. That fateful never, never looms over them like the vengeful Eumenides in a Greek tragedy.

The sentimental Lieutenant Rodé shouts from a distance: "Good-bye, Echo," while the "always satisfied" Kulygin, Masha's husband, brings out her hat and coat with a happy smile. He believes that "life runs along in a certain pattern," which fortunately has remained undisturbed this time. Masha is still with him. Vershinin is gone, his worries are all over. "Let's begin life anew, Masha," he pleads, but *"O fallacem hominem spem —* accusative case after an interjection" — he sees her distressed, angry face and finally understands that things will *never* be as they were. Two persons only remain unmoved: Natasha and the old servant Ferapont. The delightful old Ferapont is upset, he thinks the end of the world is approaching. "The hall porter from the law courts was saying just now that in the winter there were two hundred degrees of frost in St. Petersburg, he said. . . . He was saying that two thousand people were frozen to death. The people were frightened, he said . . ."

Natasha, too, that "bristly animal" — as she is described by her own husband — indifferent to the general sorrow and impervious to beauty, begins to make her practical domestic plans. "In the first place I shall have that avenue of fir trees cut down, then that maple, it is so hideous at night." And addressing Irena, she reproves her for her bad taste: "This belt does not suit you at all, my dear." But even she soon becomes silent, plunged in her utilitarian, prosaic thoughts.

Stillness prevails again. A deep nostalgia is felt, a nostalgia for distant horizons and unattainable happiness.

In *The Three Sisters* Chekhov presented the idea that the Russians were too completely maladjusted and unadapted ever to believe that there was important work to be done in their own place and time. The prewar intelligentsia were unable to accept submissively the daily routine of their duties, which appeared to them colorless and boring. Always seeking the unattainable, they displayed unpardonable weakness as soon as they were confronted with reality, a trait which, indeed, became only too obvious in the fateful years of the Revolution.

The author, as if foreseeing the sufferings which were to befall his native land, has given us the key to an understanding of the tragedy of 1917. The intelligentsia, like those in *The Three Sisters*, dreaming about Eden on earth, saw faraway, alluring mirages of the future but failed to recognize the menacing reality. And Chekhov neither judged nor moralized but remained faithful to himself. He simply stated facts with his usual objectivity.

If now, after so many years, we consider that play retrospectively and remember that it was written four years before the first Revolution (1905) we certainly cannot fail to wonder at the deep insight displayed by Chekhov in his understanding of the Russian character and at his prognosis of the "coming storms and dawning new age," which would destroy the old world. With his usual acuteness, he perceived in the midst of general blindness forces stronger than human about to shape a new generation, whose heavy steps we hear distinctly in *The Cherry Garden*.

Chekhov's contemporaries, however, received *The Three Sisters* with surprise. To them it seemed as if he were repeating his old themes, drawing again the same characters, only more weak and hopeless, changing but slightly what had already been said. The success of that play was rather indefinite, as stated by Stanislavsky himself, who remembers that only after three years did the public appreciate the "beauty of that remarkable work, where every act was a triumph."[41]

Tolstoy was very much displeased, once more asserting that he was not able to read Chekhov's drama. Many people agreed with him. A. V. Lunacharsky, who under the

[41] Feider, p. 374.

Bolsheviki regime was to be Minister of Education, wrote in *Russian Thought*: "Should we really weep with those three stupid sisters who did not know how to arrange their lives with all that which had been given to them?"[42] The break with Suvorin was also reflected in his criticism of the work. In 1900 Suvorin's attitude was still kind. On May 15, he entered in his diary: "Our meeting was pleasant. We spent a nice peaceful day, went to the cemetery." But, apparently shocked by the coolness of Anton Pavlovich, whose only friend he had been for so many years, he wrote on February 10, 1902: *"The Three Sisters* by Chekhov. Tedious, except for the first act, too many monologues, annoying in their repetition. The humor of Gogol and Ostrovsky aroused humane feelings. Here, on the contrary, the dryness suppresses and numbs them." And on September 4 of the same year, he added maliciously: "Gorky's popularity offends Chekhov's pride."

Victor Burenin, one of the principal collaborators of *Novoe Vremya*, who never liked Chekhov but was probably held in check by Suvorin, began immediately after their estrangement to attack the writer without mercy. When in 1901 in *Sievernie Tsvety* (Northern Flowers) there appeared Chekhov's story "At Night," Burenin hissed disapprovingly: "A very savory little tale. Maupassant himself would shrink from such indiscretion, but Mr. Chekhov is going further than Maupassant. . . . By the way, it is time for Mr. Chekhov to surpass Maupassant."[43]

"At Night" was based on the early story entitled "On the Sea," written in 1883. Despite the "piquancy" of the situation there is not one coarse word or risqué description. The idea of surpassing Maupassant, whom he considered one of the greatest contemporary masters, never

[42] *Russkaya Mysl'*, Number 2, 1903.
[43] *Novoe Vremya*, No. 9037, 1901.

occurred to the modest Chekhov, who on October 9, 1888, wrote to A. N. Pleshcheyev: "It seems to me I can be accused of everything, but not of the desire to appear what I am not."

Burenin naturally made fun of *The Three Sisters* and wrote a parody — *Nine Sisters and Not Even One Fiancé! What a Bedlam!* The sisters were presented as sucking a rag out of boredom and the author, acclaimed by the public, appeared, followed by tame gnats and roaches.[44] Chekhov in his early début, had printed some of his "funny tales" in the humorous papers under the headline "Gnats and Flies." Thus Burenin was also mocking the realistic interpretation of the play.

The Three Sisters did not create any sensation. Chekhov, however, was generally recognized, and those attacks could not do him any harm. A great spiritual bond attached him to the Art Theatre, where all the actors played to perfection, and in their unique interpretation the mastery of his dialogue was praised by the critics. It was noted that he knew how to convey to his audience the horror of solitude and the dismal gloom of the realization that self-satisfied inferiority is always victorious in the daily routine of life.

This mixture of criticism and approbation always unnerved and afflicted Chekhov, and since the negative verdict prevailed, his friends were glad that he was living at the time in Nice. Yet he did not long remain absent. Invariably maladjusted to his environment, Anton Pavlovich never made any effort to abide peacefully in one place. Tortured by truly pathological restlessness, he returned in February to Yalta, where his activity became more and more feverish, as is often the case with those attacked by tuberculosis. He made an appeal to Russian

[44] *Novoe Vremya*, No. 8999, 1901.

society to help the consumptive; at his native Taganrog, he organized a library and a museum. Unable to travel, consumed with nostalgia for distant horizons, he invented every day a new task or accepted new responsibilities.

The writer Alexander Kuprin, a young man then, remembers that Chekhov used to say to him: "I cannot understand why you, healthy and free as you are, do not go, for example, to Australia (Australia, for some reason, was a favorite part of the world with him) or at least to Siberia."[45] As for himself, he continuously made new plans for his future. Like Robert Louis Stevenson, he never stopped working until the end; in addition to his writing he was constantly trying to improve his form and style by reading Russian classics. Above all, he appreciated Lermontov, considering his "'Taman'" a perfect tale and his "Parus" (The Sail) a perfect piece of poetry. His aversion to "grandiloquent words" grew with every year. One day, another young writer, Bunin, who saw him quite often in Yalta, said: "Anton Pavlovich, I am just torn to pieces by reflexes." Chekhov looking at him with his observant doctor's eyes calmly answered: "Yes, you had better stop drinking vodka."[46]

In May, as the weather became warmer, Anton Pavlovich, who could not sit still, went back to Moscow. Upon arriving, he wrote a curious letter to his sister, saying (May, 1901): "Well, I have seen Dr. Shchurovsky. He found altered resonances in both lungs, and ordered me to go immediately for the cure in the province of Ufa. There, in the sanatorium, bothersome and uncomfortable, I would have to stay about two months! To go alone is bothersome, to take a cure is bothersome, to ask someone to go with me is selfish and therefore disagreeable. I would

[45] Kuprin's recollections, in *Chekhovskii sbornik*, p. 113.
[46] Bunin, V, 306.

have married, but have no documents: they all are in my desk in Yalta."

However, to the great surprise of the family, he did on May 25 marry Olga Knipper. His wedding was so secret that neither his mother nor his sister knew about it beforehand, nor even his brother, Ivan Pavlovich, who had seen him that very morning.[47]

Stanislavsky remembers that Chekhov invited several people for supper, relatives and friends, but to everybody's surprise failed to appear himself. Finally, a telegram was received in which he asked all the guests to wish him a "happy honeymoon."

Occasionally, though very seldom, the facetious Antosha Chekhonte dispossessed the stern figure of Anton Chekhov, playing innocent tricks or saying "funny" things. After his marriage, he wrote (February 26, 1903) to his friend Potapenko, who had witnessed his flirtation with Lika: "There are no particular changes. I am married. To be sure, at my age it is almost unnoticeable, just like a little baldness on my head."

This clandestine marriage may be explained by the timidity of Chekhov, who could never bear any kind of pomp or celebration — an aversion illustrated by his letter to Olga Knipper (April 18, 1901): "If you promise me that not a soul in Moscow shall know about our wedding before it has taken place, I will marry you on the very day of my arrival. Somehow I dread the ceremony, the congratulations, the champagne glass in my hand, and a vague smile on my face."

The wedding was followed by immediate departure to the sanatorium, which was situated in a beautiful oak forest. Chekhov was soon so bored by the ordeal of the cure that, despite the protests of his wife and his doctors,

[47] Mikhail Chekhov, *Anton Chekhov*, p. 148.

he stayed there only six weeks instead of the required two months. While Madame Knipper-Chekhova went to Moscow, he returned to Yalta, rather impatiently planning to write an entirely new play, quite different from anything he had ever written before.

The visit to Moscow and long talks with his friends had made this sensitive man understand that in *The Three Sisters* he had not raised any new questions and had not captured the mood of that time, which was no longer depressed and despondent. If the antithesis of "Why live?" and "We must live" appealed to some people at the appearance of *Uncle Vanya* in 1899, it was out of tune in 1901, when Russia had finally shaken off the lethargy of many decades and was facing a tremendous expansion in every phase of national life.

Radical changes were taking place, blotting out the tendencies of the previous epoch, and paving the way for new thoughts and ideals. Russia, occupying one sixth of the globe, sure of her arms and her might, was attaining the highest standards of culture and revealed her new status in a more complex and refined psychology. The unhappy, *superfluous* man, who for so many years had reflected the mood of society, was no longer the unchallenged ruler of literature. That particular type of man in constant brooding (*grübeln*), at odds with the world, lacking the conviction of reality, in love with the abstract, appeared under the influence of German philosophy, which in the '40s had invaded a large part of the intellectual circles. Turgenev, Pisemsky, Goncharov and Herzen depicted dreamy, useless people long before Chekhov.[48] The society that admired them for fifty years finally grew

[48] Pisemsky, *Boyarshchina* (1845); Herzen, *Whose Fault* (1846-1847); Turgenev, *The Diary of a Superfluous Man* (1851), and *Rudin* (1855); and Goncharov, *Oblomov* (1858) are the most characteristic novels depicting the *lishnii chelovek* (the useless, superfluous man).

tired of those idealistic misfits bereft of self-assertion and will.

Other thoughts, already nascent in 1890, with the admiration for Vladimir Soloviev and Nietzsche, began to develop with habitual Russian intensity under the aesthetic influence of Edgar Allan Poe, Baudelaire, Verlaine and Villiers de l'Isle-Adam. These authors were read with enthusiasm in the new society, which at the same time was greeting at home the rise of such men as Valerii Brusov, Alexander Blok, Andrey Bely, Dimitrii Merezhkovsky, and Viacheslav Ivanov. Highly gifted and profoundly erudite, these young writers were beginning the Symbolist movement, which presents a most complex and fascinating development in Russian letters. They believed in the complete liberation of art from all utilitarianism and had a mystic conception of beauty.

"Suffering is a great thing" was the main idea of Dostoyevsky in *Crime and Punishment* (1866). Now everybody, satiated with morbidity, believed that beauty was much greater. Numerous exquisite magazines began to appear on the market such as *Vyesy* (The Scales, 1904-1909) and *Zolotoe Runo* (The Golden Fleece, 1906-1909), which was also entitled, in French, *La Toison d'or*, and was founded by the multimillionaire, Nikolay Riabushinsky.

The search for greater refinement was felt several years before the death of Chekhov (1904). In 1899, Sergey Diagilev, the world-famous promoter of the Russian Ballet, with a group of painters including Benois, Sierov, Somov, and Nikolay Roerich (so well known in America), started the periodical *Mir Iskusstva* (The World of Art), which opened a new era in the history of art. The importance of these magazines as a deep educative influence cannot be overemphasized. D. S. Mirsky says that by "1915 Russian society was aesthetically one of the most cultivated and experienced in Europe."[49] Art has always and everywhere been the true index of culture; as demonstrating the heights to which art had risen at that time, one need merely mention a few names of great renown. In music there were Rachmaninov, Scriabin, Stravinsky, Koussevitsky; in the opera, Chaliapin, Sobinov, Nezhdanova. The Russian stage was famous for the universally acknowledged Moscow Art Theatre and for the Ballet with Karsavina, Pavlova, Nijinsky and hundreds of outstanding dancers. Russia lived an intense artistic life of which the offshots alone, the graceful bagatelles, have charmed the outside world for years — for example Baliev's *Chauve-Souris* with its "Katin'ka," and "The Wooden Soldiers."

Russian boys and girls filled the universities at home. Numbers of them were found in France and in Germany as well as in the art schools of Italy. They brought back new thoughts and ideas, thus creating that charming cosmopolitanism so attractive among the Russian intelligentsia. Indeed, it was the beginning of a different epoch, and Chekhov felt that he had to adapt himself to changed currents and to write another play as a counterpoise to the gloomy picture of *The Three Sisters*.

All buttoned up in his heavy coat, despite the Crimean heat, Chekhov loved to sit on a bench hidden by oleanders and roses he had himself planted in times past. For long days he could now gaze at the sparkling Black Sea, which in its steady murmur told him tales of another life, beautiful, serene, and eternal. What fleeting images were coursing then through his feverish mind? Who can picture the capricious arabesques of his thoughts when his tired eyes

[49] Mirsky, *Contemporary Russian Literature*, p. 155.

wandered from mountains to gardens, resting on the green lace of the southern vegetation, on the slender cypresses which like large, dark cones stood up against the purity of the limpid blue sky? It seems that his wounded soul, almost relieved from the burden of matter, lulled by the beauty and peace of this luminous nature all blended with sunshine and glory, had experienced at last the blissful sensation of freedom, a freedom from objective realities of life.

Weary of struggle like his heroes, he surrendered to the inevitable and accepted with smiling indifference his swiftly approaching death. He knew that for him recovery was impossible and he dismissed care for his health as no longer necessary. He conceived of the idea of parting with Yalta, of going back to Moscow, to the Art Theatre, to Olga Knipper, that gifted, interesting woman who gave him the happiness he had never known before.

On October 1, 1902, Chekhov wrote to Stanislavsky: "I shall be in Moscow on October 15 and shall explain why my play [*The Cherry Garden*] is not yet written. I have already a theme. . . . In Lubimovka [property of Stanislavsky's mother, near Moscow] I felt very well; it could not have been better. Upon coming to Yalta I was taken ill, began to cough, could not eat for about a month. Now I am feeling well again. The physician who examined me found a great change for the better. It means that the climate of Lubimovka and my fishing (from morning until evening) were helpful despite the fact that it rained all summer."

"Chekhov, an intelligent man, could say strange, absurd words when the conversation concerned Moscow," as his colleague, Doctor S. Elpatievsky, recalled. Once when the doctor was persuading him not to visit Moscow in Octo-

CHEKHOV'S BIRTHPLACE AT TAGANROG

CHEKHOV'S RETREAT AT YALTA

ber, Anton Pavlovich explained in all seriousness that the air of this city was especially good and vivifying for him and that medical men should avoid getting into ruts because " 'even the bad October weather might be beneficial to some with diseased lungs.' . . . Everything was dear to his heart in Moscow, people and streets and the chimes of various Nicholases, 'Nicholas the Wet' and 'Nicholas on the Wood Strip,'[50] and the typical Moscow cabdriver and all Moscow harum-scarum. Scarcely would his condition be relieved by a sojourn in Yalta than he would begin to talk about returning to Moscow, where his illness would invariably be aggravated."[51]

Evtikhii Karpov, the unlucky stage director of the Alexandrine Theatre, described thus his last meeting with Chekhov in Moscow in the house of Vera Kommissarzhevskaya (the well-known actress who played Nina in *The Sea Gull* at its unfortunate opening) : "He entered breathing heavily and said in a hoarse, breaking voice — 'Good Morning.' His face was livid with fatigue. . . . His eyes wearily gazed into space.

" 'Are you writing something?' asked Madame Kommissarzhevskaya.

" 'Yes, I am,' answered Chekhov with a timid smile. 'But I am not writing what I should like to write. My writings have become tedious. Something else is necessary now.'

" 'What, pray?'

" 'Something entirely different . . . something cheerful and strong . . . We have outlived the gray dawdle. There is a turn in public opinion . . . a sharp turn . . . I as-

[50] Saint Nicholas was one of the most popular saints in Russia. In Moscow alone, forty-one churches were dedicated in his honor. Many of them had very curious names, such as "Nicholas on the Chicken Feet."

[51] Elpatievsky, in *Chekhovskii sbornik*, p. 47.

sure you, here in the capital it is not noticeable, but in the South the movement is strong.'

"He rose. 'Do you understand me? I should like to catch this cheerful mood . . . to write a play . . . a cheerful play; perhaps I shall.' "[52]

On December 12, 1903, in the *Journal dlia Vsiekh* (The Magazine for All) there appeared the last story by Chekhov, "Nievesta" (The Betrothed). For the first time we see an independent, courageous girl, Nadya Shumina, who rebels against the dreariness of idle life and leaves for the university, to the dismay of her mother and her grandmother. Alexander, a friend of her childhood days, persuades her to go "because only educated, unselfish people are necessary; they alone will bring the kingdom of heaven on earth."

While Nadya happily turns a new page of her life, the consumptive Alexander (like Chekhov himself in 1901) goes to the sanatorium and there he dies. Before he leaves, he hears the watchman's rattle — *tok, tok.* And time indeed, like an inexorable watchman, rattled threateningly over the dying Chekhov. This introduction of sounds, as has been mentioned, became his favorite impressionistic method. Stanislavsky, before he learned the theme of his new play, always asked what sound effects he intended to use.

Early in the fall of 1903 Anton Pavlovich finished his last play. As usual he claimed that *The Cherry Garden* "was not a drama, but a comedy, sometimes even a farce." In letters to his wife he said (September 21, 1903) : "The last act is gay, the whole play is gay, light." And on September 25: "By the way, there is not one shot." In four of his previous plays, as we know, shots had been an

[52] Feider, p. 417.

ntegral part of the plot: Ivanov kills himself; so does Treplev; Uncle Vanya fires at Professor Serebriakov; and n *The Three Sisters* Baron Tuzenbach is killed in a duel.

Chekhov continued to write to his wife, showing great anxiety. On September 27: "I wired you that the play was finished, the four acts being written. . . . The characters are lifelike; but what the play in itself may be, I don't know." And on October 19: "Yesterday I did not write to you because I was waiting nervously for the telegram. Last night came your wire, this morning another from Vladimir Ivanovich [Nemirovich] — one hundred and eighty words. I was anxious, fearful, especially about the static character of the student Trofimov. . . . Is my play going to be accepted? If yes, then when? I shall come early in November."

To Nemirovich he wrote (October 23) : "Why did you wire that there were many weeping people in my play? Where are they? Only Varya weeps because it is her nature. Her tears should not evoke sadness in the audience. . . . I often say 'tearfully' but it merely indicates the mood of the *dramatis personae*, not real tears. There is no cemetery in the second act."

Anton Pavlovich lived in agonies of fear that his play would again be misunderstood: "I am writing about life . . . this is a gray everyday life indeed . . . but not an eternal whimpering. They always interpret me as a lachrymose writer, yet I have written several volumes of gay stories; why then do the critics represent me as a weeper?"[53]

He declared that *The Cherry Garden* was misunderstood by Stanislavsky and Nemirovich themselves: "Why on the posters and in the advertisements is my play so persistently called a *drama*? Nemirovich and Stanislavsky

[53] Recollections of Evtikhii Karpov, in Feider, p. 450.

see in it a meaning different from what I intended. They
never read it attentively, I am sure."[54]

The anxiety and even the grumbling of Anton Pavlovich were wholly unjustified this time. Upon reading *The
Cherry Garden*, Constantine Stanislavsky proclaimed it a
masterpiece, and this was sufficient for the ultimate success of the play. Originally a gifted amateur and a propa-
gator of the new form of dramatic art, Constantine
Stanislavsky had become one of its greatest authorities —
a famous actor and stage director of the Moscow Art
Theatre, which had already gained general recognition.
He and Nemirovich were no longer laughed at as "simpletons seized with frenzy." They were great artists producing
remarkable work. Their profound admirer, the well-known
Moscow Maecenas, Savva Morosov, one of the richest men
in Russia, displeased with the old Hermitage, entrusted
the architect Schechtel with the construction of a new theatre for them. This munificence was universally acclaimed.

There was something stimulating in the air of those
days. The road of the good old Russian Empire seemed
to be paved with might and glory. Art flourished amid
apparent harmony and peace. And Savva Morosov, not
foreseeing the thunderstorms, the first peals of which were
to be heard in the guns of the Russo-Japanese War (1904-
1905), worked in shirt-sleeves from morning to evening
in the theatre. His enthusiasm was so great that his
brother Sergey, another multimillionaire, was carried away
by it and helped him like a journeyman. In blissful
ignorance, they could not imagine that in less than two
decades they and their like would be forced to work for
shelter and bread.

The new building in the Kamergersky Alley was soon
ready. It was equipped with all the technical improve-

[54] Chekhov to Madame Knipper-Chekhova, April 10, 1904.

ments necessary for the new form of dramatic art. With subdued lights and with sea gulls beautifully outlined on the gray, separating curtains, it was introduced to the public as the Chekhov Theatre and officially opened October 25, 1902.

XIII

Sunset in the Cherry Garden

THE prevailing current of thought at the beginning of
the new century was aestheticism. Born in the preceding
decade under the overwhelming influence of Nietzsche
and the famous Russian philosopher, Vladimir Soloviev,
it was a mighty factor in transforming society. This new
ideal, however, did not obliterate the revolutionary movement, which for seventy-five years produced an uninterrupted series of outbursts and suppressions.

The Decembrist Revolt was crushed by the iron hand
of Nikolay I. With the withdrawal of the nobility from
political life and the rise of the *rasnochintsy*, the subterranean activity reappeared in the form of *Narodnaya
Volya* (Will of the People) , which led to the assassination
of Alexander II and was followed again by a powerful
reaction. At the same time, the tremendous growth of
Russian capitalism had for its immediate counterbalance
the development of Marxism, which marked the end of
rural Russia and freed the social consciousness from outworn populist ideas. Thus began the era of *Dialectic
Materialism*, a philosophy based on the teachings of Marx
and Engels, representing the world as undergoing perpetual transformations and changes and human history as
evolving under immutable natural laws in which the will

of man has no part whatsoever. Since nothing remains still, nothing is worthy of worship; "the only objective reality is matter which is outside man, but is reflected in the mind of man," said Lenin, who in middle of the '90s was beginning his career as a newspaperman.[55]

The scientific aspect of the new doctrine appealed to the radical intelligentsia, heirs of the "thinking realists" of the '60s, who accepted it *de plano*. When the general discontent with the Russo-Japanese War reached its peak, they rallied their forces in the mighty Revolution of 1905. This was also suppressed. Its spirit remained apparently dormant until twelve years later when the last wave, most formidable of all, swept the old regime from the face of the earth.

Chekhov did not live to witness the first revolution, but his keen intuition enabled him to foresee coming events and to hear the clang of arms amid the general worship of beauty. He realized that the present peace was merely stillness in the air before a great storm. In his *Note-Books* we find this amazing sentence: "It seems to me that we — worn-out, stereotyped, banal people — have grown quite moldy. While we intellectuals are rummaging among old rags and biting each other according to the dear Russian custom, something is boiling around us. There is a life of which we know nothing. Great events will take us unaware, like sleeping fairies."[56]

Chekhov's last play, *The Cherry Garden,* not only sums up all his previous work but also shows an acute perception of the hidden currents of his epoch, pregnant with the imminent danger of general collapse. Yet Anton Pavlovich displayed an unaccustomed cheerfulness, as if realiz-

[55] Gurev, *Malaya Sovietskaya Encyclopedia* (The Little Soviet Encyclopedia) , II, 856.
[56] Chekhov, *Note-Books,* p. 79.

ing that he had nothing more to say, that he could not change the course of destiny. It appears that he was gaining in the happiness of his personal life that nervous equilibrium he had never possessed. When he moved to Moscow for the winter of 1903-1904 he was in that sunny state of mind which none had noticed in him since the days of Antosha Chekhonte. On November 19, 1903, he wrote to Kign, one of his numerous acquaintances: "I married and am very glad I did. It seems to me that my life has changed for the better."

Unconcerned with his health, which rapidly declined in the harsh northern winter, he still received his many visitors, this time without complaining that they disturbed him. Though his life work was finished, he was ardently interested in everything that was going on. While he himself maintained silence, he listened attentively to conversations, his kind doctor's eyes scrutinizing all the faces about him.

The actors of the Art Theatre came almost daily. They were at that time learning their parts, anxious to give *The Cherry Garden* on Chekhov's birthday, January 17, 1904, which coincided with the silver jubilee of his literary career. Anton Pavlovich, despite his constant fever, attended all rehearsals at the request of Constantine Stanislavsky, who considered this play very hard to set, because its charm lay "in its elusive, subtle fragrance."

Indeed, light and ethereal, woven like lace, it is the most complex of all Chekhov's works. Three years had elapsed since the production of *The Three Sisters*, a drama of stifling provincial life which left the gloomy impression of low horizons and autumnal haze. The author had found new ways for fuller and richer artistic expression. The cheerful note which resounded in the air made him write *The Cherry Garden* in a major key, yet its melodic cadence is still tinged with melancholy. Its theme may be traced to Chekhov's youth, to the summers he spent in the province of Khar'kov where Nikolay, his favorite brother, had died. The dilapidated estate of Luka had inspired this poem of an entire epoch in its passing. This is a final chord to his beloved *leit-motif*, the disintegration of old Russia and the rise of new people, represented in Lopakhin. The characters, as if wrapped in light gauze, aimlessly swaying to and fro, retain their Chekhovian elusiveness and seem to be called to life by the will of a magician.

The musical structure of *The Cherry Garden* suggests the fresh and Nordic melodies of Grieg. Of the silver and brown colors of his palette so skillfully used previously, the author kept only the silver shades. His autumn was ended. This is the cool, crisp morning of a winter day, the winter of Chekhov, which the radiant spring with its dawns, its brooks, and its warm breeze will never know again. This is the last farewell to life. "It is close on sunrise, it is May. The cherry trees are in flower, but it is chilly in the garden. There is an early frost." Through the windows one can see white blossoms which cover the trees like snow, and for the first and the last time we enter that silvery world under the rays of the *rising* sun, the sun Anton Chekhov loved to greet in the vast steppes of the Don, in the forests of Siberia, on the banks of the Amur and the Yenissey.

In *The Cherry Garden*, which may be regarded as a dramatized novelette, the author shows us again inner tragedies, unnoticeable on the surface. Love intrigue is completely excluded, and the mutual relationship of the characters remains the same at the end as it was at the beginning. Apparently nothing important has happened. Weak, inefficient people are about to lose their property.

What of it? They never cared for their cherry garden. Yet the loss of it is the greatest disaster that could possibly befall them. It is a moral shock rather than a financial catastrophe.

Madame Ranevskaya (the owner), whose life is nothing but a permanent conflict between mind and heart, has spent several years in Paris, where she has wrecked her fortune by unpardonable extravagance. With her daughter Anya, she returns to her home, the most conspicuous feature of which is the large cherry garden adjoining it. Unfortunately she has no more money to take care of her estate. The practical merchant Lopakhin suggests cutting down the cherry trees and selling the property in lots. Madame Ranevskaya is indignant. Her garden is the most beautiful thing in the whole province, and she, who for years has deserted her estate, feels now that she loves it and cannot be separated from it. It epitomizes not only her home but her country; it is from now on her last abode, where she has planned to lead a peaceful, idyllic existence, as if it were the hamlet of Trianon. Of course it never occurs to her to take some decisive action to save it. She merely waits indolently and weeps. As with all Chekhovian characters, her keyed-up emotions are always expressed in tears which flow on every occasion; her soul "is shaken at every sound."

Her brother Gaev comes to see her and both exultantly greet the old house, every piece of furniture. While Ranevskaya repeats in ecstasy: "My dear nursery, oh, my beautiful room," and kisses her cupboard with an exclamation, "My dear little cupboard!" Gaev salutes the old bookcase, "My dear, most respected bookcase," exactly as in *The Three Sisters* the young Lieutenant Rodé bade farewell to the echo — a situation ridiculous but somehow fitting to those naïve dreamers, who, despite their incongruity, are infinitely superior to the rising new people, energetic, clever and hard. Gaev is just as kind and absurd as his sister. He belongs to the vast majority of the Russian gentry, ready to embrace the universe but not able to make any decision or to show any will power. To a lesser degree than the "three sisters," Gaev and Ranevskaya still bear traces of that neurasthenia which characterized the intellectual elite of the Chekhovian era.

Madame Ranevskaya is pleased to find her household, among whom we see the unforgettable Firs, an old footman aged eighty-seven, who, like the unique servant types of the previous generation depicted by Goncharov, is the soul of love and faithfulness. For him life without his masters is inconceivable: "I will go wherever you order me to go." He sincerely regards the emancipation of the serfs as a "catastrophe." Exquisite is Duniasha, the coquettish maid, who recalls a graceful French soubrette of the eighteenth century. She is infatuated with Yasha, the butler, who has just arrived from Paris, but he only yawns and speaks about "his soul's deep restlessness." Duniasha loves to faint, and her delicacy makes a great impression on the clerk, Epikhodov, an unlucky man nicknamed "twenty-two misfortunes." Never separated from his guitar, he sings touching songs on every occasion. The language he uses in conversation with her is curiously involved: "Undoubtedly, perhaps, you may be right. But certainly if you regard the matter from that aspect, then you, if I may say so, and you must excuse my candor, have absolutely reduced me to a state of mind." Duniasha listens impatiently, powders her face, and asks for a respite. "Please leave me alone now, I am meditating." The part of Epikhodov in the original cast was acted by Moskvin, one of the greatest Russian comedians. Together with several other minor characters, he presents that comic element which Chekhov introduces for the first time into his plays.

Varya, the housekeeper and Madame Ranevskaya's adopted daughter, tries in vain to persuade her that their financial situation is really most serious. Varya is a sort of Cassandra who is believed by no one. Deeply devoted to her adopted family, she presents a curious combination of great efficiency with a purely Russian trait — a desire to go, to be free of the bothersome routine of her duties: "All day long I am looking after the house and thinking all the time that I would go away somewhere all by myself . . . to Kiev . . . to Moscow . . . from one holy place to another. And I would tramp and tramp and that would be splendid."

An especially significant character is Lopakhin, a powerful example of the new Russian, toned down by Chekhov so that he combines hard practical common sense with a realization of other, less material values. "Oh, Lord, you gave us great forests, endless fields, and infinite horizons, and we, living here, should be giants in truth." He is to buy the cherry garden. His attitude towards Ranevskaya is a strange mixture of shrewdness and gentleness.

Masterfully sketched is the tramp who recites the poetry of Nekrasov: "Brother, my suffering brother." He is a little drunk and frightens Varya by asking her for alms: "Mademoiselle, please give a hungry Russian about thirty kopeks." Lopakhin is irritated and chases him away, but Ranevskaya, although completely ruined, gives him a gold piece: "Take this, there is no silver. It does not matter. Take this gold piece."

She is without doubt extravagant but typical of her class and her epoch. Chekhov is highly ingenious in contrasting the full-blooded, calculating peasant, Lopakhin, with the impractical, inefficient gentry, sunk in revery.

"They all are thoughtful and still, it is quiet. . . . Suddenly a distant sound is heard as if from the sky, the sound of the breaking string, sadly dying away." This strange, sad sound frightens the nervous Ranevskaya. It is a symbol of a coming misfortune, which is near, very near, almost at hand.

In the third act Ranevskaya still has not paid the interest on her mortgaged property, which is to be sold at auction. She expects the impending catastrophe every minute, yet still clings to a childish hope that something will happen to prevent it. As a means of diversion she gives a ball, and while she waits for news, she dances and dances to the music of a cheap band.

Firs is the only one who appears to be aware of how ludicrous this situation is: "At our balls some time back generals, barons, and admirals used to dance; now we have post-office clerks and station-masters, and even they come as a favor." In the great white ballroom they waltz, like grotesque marionettes pulled by invisible strings, and fail to hear the steps of menacing destiny. Lopakhin enters. He has bought the cherry garden. He, the son of a serf, is the only master of this beautiful estate. Now he can do whatever he wishes. In this Russian nature, formed amidst "endless fields . . . and infinite horizons," all feelings are boundless like the wide expanse of his native land. And he, the dignified, sedate Lopakhin, shouts in wild joy: "Wait, ladies and gentlemen, my head is going around, I can't talk . . . The cherry garden is mine now . . . mine. My God, my God . . . the cherry garden is mine! Tell me I am drunk or mad or dreaming . . . if my father and my grandfather could rise from their graves and look at the whole affair, and see how their Ermolai, their beaten and uneducated Ermolai, who used to run barefoot in the winter, how that very Ermolai has bought an estate which is the most beautiful thing in the world; I've bought the estate where my grandfather and my father were slaves, where they were not even allowed in the kitchen," and addressing the band: "Musicians, play. I want to hear you! Come and look at Ermolai Lopakhin laying his ax to the cherry garden."

There are many destructive traits in his complex nature, but first of all Lopakhin is a Chekhov character, subdued by the delicate mastery of the author's touch. This coarse peasant is kind and feels a deep compassion for the weeping Ranevskaya, which he expresses in caressing words: "My dear, my poor one . . . (he weeps) . . . Oh, if only the whole thing were done with, if only our uneven, unhappy life were different." But then, with the sudden change of mood, so apparent in Russian music and in Russian dance and so artfully brought out by Chekhov, Lopakhin, turning to the band, adds unexpectedly: "Musicians, play nicely! Go on, do just as I want you to do. The new owner is coming, the owner of the cherry garden."

In vain Anya tries to comfort her broken mother: "You are crying, my dear mother, my beautiful mother . . . You still have your wonderful, pure soul . . . Come with me, away from here, come. We will plant a new garden, finer than this. You will see it, and you will understand . . . a deep joy will sink into your soul like the evening sun and you will smile, mother. Come, let's go."

The student Trofimov, a former tutor of Madame Ranevskaya's little son who was drowned several years ago, still lives in her hospitable house. He regards the cherry garden as a symbol of old Russia and expresses, like a "repentant nobleman," his thoughts of suffering and redemption: "In order to begin to live in the present, we must first redeem the past, and that can be done only by suffering, by strenuous, uninterrupted labor." When Varya suspects him of being in love with Anya, he exclaims in indignation at such vulgarity: "We are above love." The purpose of their lives is "to escape petty and deceptive things which prevent them from being happy and free." Facing the unknown, this young idealist does not accept the money generously offered to him by the rich Lopakhin: "Even if you gave me twenty thousand rubles I should refuse. I am a free man! And all the things that you people, rich or poor, value so highly and so dearly have no influence over me. Mankind goes on to the highest truths and to the highest happiness possible on earth." And he welcomes the new life: "There it comes, it moves nearer and nearer, I hear its steps already. If we do not see it and are not to know it, what does that matter? All Russia is our garden. The land is great and beautiful." Anya, who considers Trofimov to be the best man in the world, repeats after him in youthful exuberance: "Good-bye, home! Good-bye, old life."

An exquisite gentleness emanates from the ethereal lightness of the play. The characters speak to each other with the greatest kindness, in caressing and friendly words. Lopakhin says: "I want to tell something very pleasant, very delightful to you." Duniasha, the maid, claims: "I simply love words of tenderness." All of them are generous and give freely whatever they have. They often weep, even Lopakhin, but they never quarrel, are never angry. Ranevskaya, despite her overwhelming grief, never loses her temper. She simply cries: "Oh, my dear, my sweet, beautiful garden!" Like Chekhov himself, she bids farewell to life, "My life, my youth, my happiness, good-bye."

Their existence will hardly know glamorous adventure.

The rich Lopakhins, the *kulaks*,[57] are most certainly ruined. The Gaevs have lost everything. Varya works somewhere and dreams, in great secrecy, about travel to holy places; Trofimov tries to adapt himself to the new conditions in the hope of a future happiness for humanity. And the Ranevskys, what do the Ranevskys do? They sell dresses in the shops of the Champs-Elysées or Fifth Avenue, or teach foreign languages if they are educated.

They all are gone to other problems and other sorrows, forgetting the faithful aged Firs who, true to himself, is neither vexed nor offended. He only worries about Gaev, that big careless boy. Who will remind him to keep warm in the evening? And Firs, in distress, wanders like a shadow through the empty rooms which his masters have left forever. The thin threads which attach the old man to life are severed. "Life is gone as if I had never lived." "The emptiness is felt. It is quiet. Firs lies down motionless. Silence follows. Only one sound of the ax falling on a tree is heard somewhere away in the garden."

These are the very last words that Chekhov wrote. The cherry garden is destroyed; its former proprietors have left, and the ax will keep falling until the tremendous, mysterious force behind that ax wears out, and on the debris of the past the new owner will begin a new cycle of life.

On January 17, 1904, his last birthday and the twenty-fifth anniversary of his literary career, Anton Pavlovich was present at the first performance of *The Cherry Garden*, which proved to be a tremendous success, and was considered an important event in the artistic life of Moscow. The Chekhov Theatre had surpassed itself. The roles were given to Stanislavsky (Gaev), Knipper (Ranevskaya),

---

[57] *Kulak* — a term of contempt denoting a rich but unscrupulous peasant, a sort of "skinflint."

Kachalov (Trofimov), Lilina (Anya), Andreeva (Varya), Artem (Firs), and Moskvin (Epikhodov), and other brilliant actors. They knew how to convey to the public the inner tragedy hidden by the apparent trifles of life. With supreme art, they combined great gentleness and a tension as of impending, unavoidable doom. One got the impression of sliding somewhere in a cold, bare space, devoid of all protection, exposed to winds and storms, while the safety of the old home with its cozy fireplace and familiar things was left behind forever. The "emptiness was felt" and Constantine Stanislavsky remembers that, for some time, gloom prevailed in the theatre, soon to be interrupted by thunderous applause. Chekhov himself, deathly pale and thin, received an enthusiastic ovation.

His weakness was so obvious that some charitable persons in the audience cried out to him: "Take a seat." Chekhov frowned and remained standing during all the endless speeches. He was extremely sad amid all the noise and shouting, which this time was not meant to humiliate him as on the dreadful night of *Chaika* (The Sea Gull) but to show approval and admiration.

Only once a pale smile appeared on his tired face, when one of the speakers addressed him as "Dear, most respected Anton Pavlovich."[58] He cast a sidelong glance towards Stanislavsky, who, as Gaev, had greeted the old, worn bookcase with the same words. As he went home, followed by general cheering, there was in his soul only deep regret over a recognition which had come so late that he had no more strength to enjoy it.

The efforts of those past weeks had been too great. Chekhov wrote with relief to L. B. Sredin, on January 20, 1904: "The long-drawn-out proceeding with the play is finished. Now I can sit at my desk in peace and write to

[58] Stanislavsky, pp. 359-69.

you. Moscow is a nice city; at least it seems to be so this winter when I am almost well. But there is such a crush here, I have not a minute to myself, so I am dreaming of the Yalta Penates with pleasure."

For three long months Chekhov remained in Moscow. This was an ordeal! In perfect cheerfulness he departed for the dreaded Crimea, undisturbed by the separation from family and friends. The moods of that feminine soul always defied logic.

It would, however, be unjust not to mention that the Russo-Japanese War upset him greatly. He did not belong to the category of his compatriots who believed that Russian arms were invincible, and that peace would be restored in "three or four months." Chekhov watched with growing consternation the "Japanese Macacos" mercilessly slapping the "Russian Bear." If he did not live to see the surrender of Port Arthur, and the catastrophes of Mukden and Tsushima, where the Russian fleet and the Russian army were defeated, he nevertheless felt, with his usual keenness of perception, that the destiny of his fatherland was to be decided in the Far East, and that the unlucky war of 1904-1905 had initiated the disintegration of the great Russian Empire — the "colossus with feet of clay."

His correspondence as usual reflects his preoccupation. On April 13, 1904, he wrote from Yalta to Alexander Amfiteatrov, a journalist and author of humorous tales: "Should I be in good health in July or August I shall go to the Far East, not as a newspaperman, but as a physician. I believe that a physician will see more than a newspaperman."

The project concerning the Far East was, however, soon forgotten. From a letter to his wife (April 15) we learn that his health took again a turn for the worse. His medical consultants decided that he should go to Badenweiler, a German watering resort in the Schwarzwald. Again Anton Pavlovich had to cross Russia from Yalta to Moscow, where he was to meet his wife and prepare for his last journey abroad. Constantine Stanislavsky records: "We all were anxious to see him often, but his health did not always permit him to receive us. Despite his illness, his cheerfulness did not forsake him. He was showing great interest in Maeterlinck's play, which was in preparation. As for himself, he was thinking of writing another drama on a theme quite new for him: two friends love the same woman; this situation creates jealousy and tension; at last they both go on an expedition to the north pole; at the end, the two men see a white shadow sliding over the snow . . . the soul of the woman they loved, who had died far away in their native land."[59]

This highly symbolic play was never written. It was probably a passing fancy on the part of Chekhov. Some of his other friends record that he was fully aware of his desperate condition and on the eve of his departure said: "I am going away to die. All is finished. Good-bye. We shall never meet again."[60] These were words he loved to put in the mouths of his heroes.

On June 3, 1904, Anton Pavlovich left Moscow, which he was never again to see. He went to Germany with his wife. Madame Knipper-Chekhova proved to be a most devoted nurse to this restless patient, who, after they reached Badenweiler, seemed to be greatly relieved. The mountains, the flower gardens, the German cleanliness and order pleased Anton Pavlovich at first. He wrote to his mother (June 13, 1904) one of those astounding letters which are invariably perplexing; did he really believe what he was writing or was it his wish not to worry the old lady? "My dear Mother . . . my health is getting

[59] Stanislavsky, pp. 359-61.   [60] Feider, p. 453.

better and better. It looks as though I might be completely recovered in a week. There is quiet here, much sunshine, no heat."

Soon, however, his wanderlust returned, although he retained his good spirits. Unable to travel because of the vigilance of his wife and his doctors, he continually changed his residence. From his hotel he moved to "Villa Fredericke," a private house in the midst of a large garden. For a while Chekhov was satisfied, but after a few rainy days, during which he was confined to his rooms, he decided to leave. "I am now planning to quit. We shall go to Yalta by way of Trieste or some other port," he wrote to his sister on June 25.

His wife persuaded him to stay for a little while and they moved again to the Hotel Sommer. Chekhov enjoyed his new room, especially his balcony, where he would sit for hours and watch people passing. The psychology of the crowd always interested him. Yet even this occupation proved to be desperately boring. Now he began to complain about the heat. "I am suffocating and am making plans to leave. I do want to go by boat from Trieste to Odessa. It would be a wonderful trip for me." And explaining to his sister why he should prefer to go by boat rather than by rail (June 28, 1904), he added: "Besides, by railroad I shall arrive too soon and I have not yet traveled to my heart's content." This was written four days before his death. The vitality of Anton Pavlovich, who had been dying for the last five years, was truly amazing. No one foresaw that the end was so near. Doctor Schwöhrer, a specialist, came to see him every day. He was very fond of his patient and was fated to close the cycle of suffering and sorrow begun twenty-seven years before in the steppe of the Don, where another German,

Doctor Strümpf, attended Chekhov at the beginning of his illness.

On July 1, Anton Pavlovich told his wife stories so amusing that she failed to hear the gong and missed her dinner. It seemed as though the gay Antosha Chekhonte were making his last appearance on earth. The evening passed cheerfully and when Chekhov went to sleep he looked much better. Late at night, however, Madame Knipper-Chekhova, who was napping on the couch nearby, heard a strange noise. She leaped to her feet. Chekhov was suffocating. His discomfort was so great that, for the first time in his life, he asked that a doctor be sent for. Two Russian students, awakened by Madame Chekhova, went hurriedly to fetch the physician.

Soon Doctor Schwöhrer arrived, accompanied by his assistant. They sent for oxygen. Chekhov smiled: "It will come too late." A few moments later he became delirious. He spoke about the war and Russian sailors in Japan. This great humanitarian remained true to himself to the end. It was not his family or his friends on whom his last thoughts were centered: it was on Russia and her people.

Presently he regained consciousness, although his pulse was failing rapidly. The physicians gave him some champagne. Chekhov smiled again, and then in a distant whisper said: *"Ich sterbe"* (I am dying). He sank on his left side. All was ended. Two silent men bent over the motionless form, and, in the stillness of the July night, one could hear only the sobs of a lonely woman.

Chekhov was buried in Moscow beside his father and the poet Pleshcheyev in Novodevichii Convent, the golden cupolas of which, outlined against the gray northern sky, he had seen from his room in Professor Ostroumov's private hospital. At last he found an eternal abode in the cemetery he loved to visit during his lifetime because every dark poplar, every tombstone, faded flowers, and autumnal leaves "breathe pardon, sadness, and peace."

Thousands of people in St. Petersburg and Moscow were waiting to bid farewell to the author of *The Cherry Garden*. But fate once more played a grotesque joke on him. His body was brought to Russia in a railroad carriage used previously for the transportation of oysters. What an excellent theme this would have been for the writer of the *Parti-Colored Stories*, the gay and mirth-loving Antosha Chekhonte.

CHEKHOV died. He had gone to the abysmal mystery — to the exciting secret that no wisdom has ever unraveled on earth. He had completed his task. He had spoken his last word in *The Cherry Garden*. His writing reflects with unusual precision fifty years of Russian history, the collective psychology of his time. And yet he stands apart from any time in his ability to disclose the essentials of a situation, to fathom the enigma of the human heart, to grasp the restlessness of the human spirit. He is not a painter of life, he is life itself in its complex manifestations.[61]

It is fascinating to observe the gay and bubbling Antosha Chekhonte metamorphose into the silent and sad Anton Chekhov with his artistic approach to reality that paved the way to the aesthetic revival and freed the human ego from the slavery of outworn thoughts. He lived in years of transformation and crisis in the public consciousness. His literary activity began about the time of Dostoyevsky's death (1881). It seems as though Chekhov had

[61] Chekhov's value has been universally acknowledged. He has been translated into all European languages, and even into Japanese. According to D. S. Mirsky the English are his greatest admirers.

inherited the idealistic spirit of that great humanitarian and his deep love for mankind. In Dostoyevsky, however, this love was saturated with the despair of the chained Prometheus, indignant at injustice and misery. Chekhov is the kindly Uncle Vanya, whose observing doctor's eyes are fixed on us in exquisite gentleness.

Chekhov is primarily adult. He has a grown-up mind. He reveals to us the secret of thinking in abstract concepts and artistic images, thus showing a harmonious blend of literary culture and scientific training. He teaches us sincerity, "the dislike of affectation for which modern literature has the great Russian novelist to thank."[62] Profoundly intelligent himself, he often represents people of deep intelligence and intense inner life but with no capacity for self-expression. He, a great artist, understands that only the unspoken has eternal reality. In the reticence of his dialogue, in faint music or the sound of a falling ax amid complete stillness, he conveys the mystery of silence saturated with hidden potentialities, more eloquent than action itself.

He sensed in the air the end of our cycle of life. He felt the pangs of the old, presaging the birth of the new. He foresaw the hordes of humanity who have lost their cherry garden and have not yet found the road to their "Moscow." He watched the misery of struggling man — accidental creation of a blind but prolific nature, obliged to live in this deceiving world. And Chekhov pities the "lonely stranger," misled by our stepmother the earth, while he himself discerns in the silvery beam of the moon, in the fragrance of flowers, in the gentle whisper of the wind, the eternal process of destruction, separation, and death. He murmurs to all those whose path has crossed his own: *Farewell, we part and never meet again!*

[62] Gerhardi, p. 5.

Bibliography

Al'bov, V. "Dva momenta v rasvitii tvorchestva Antona Pavlovicha Chekhova" (Two Phases in the Creative Development of Anton Pavlovich Chekhov), in *Mir Bozhii*, Jan., 1903, pp. 84-115.

Alpers, B. V. Teatr revolutsii (The Theatre of the Revolution). Moscow, 1928.

Annenski, I. F. Drama nastroenii (The Drama of Moods). St. Petersburg, 1906.

Antoine, André. Mes Souvenirs sur le théâtre Antoine et sur l'Odéon, Volume I. Paris, 1928.

Arsenyev, K. "Maxim Maximovich Kovalevsky," in *Viestnik Evropy*, April, 1916, pp. 6-11.

Balukhaty, S. Problemy dramaticheskago analysa (Problems of Dramatic Analysis). Leningrad, 1927.

Beeson, B. Barker. "Anton Tchekhov, a Résumé of His Works and His Career," in *Annals of Medical History*, new series, III, 603-18 (1931).

Brandes, Georg. "Friedrich Nietzsche," in *Russkaya Mysl'*, XI, 130-53; XII, 143-61 (1900).

Budde, Evgenii. "Osnovnaya idea khudozhestvennyk proisvedenii Chekhova" (The Main Idea of the Works of Chekhov), in *Russkaya Mysl'*, Jan., 1906, pp. 1-29.

Bulgakov, Sergey. "Chekhov kak myslitel" (Chekhov as Thinker), in *Novy Put'*, Number 10, pp. 32-54; Number 11, pp. 138-52 (1904).

Bunin, Ivan. Sochinenia (Works). Marks edition. Petrograd, 1915.

Caro, E. Le Pessimisme au xixe siècle. Paris, 1878.

Chekhov, Alexander (pseudonym, A. S-Oi). "Chekhov

pievchii" (Chekhov the Singer), in *Viestnik Evropy*, Oct., 1907, pp. 825-34.

—— "Anton Pavlovich Chekhov lavochnik" (Chekhov the Shopkeeper), in *Viestnik Evropy*, Nov., 1908, pp. 190-224.

Chekhov, Anton Pavlovich. The Letters of Anton Pavlovitch Tchekov to Olga Leonardovna Knipper, translated by Constance Garnett. New York, 1926.

—— The Note-Books of Anton Tchekhov, together with Reminiscences of Tchekhov by Maxim Gorky translated by S. S. Koteliansky and Leonard Woolf. London, 1921.

—— Pis'ma (Letters), edited by his sister, Maria Chekhova. St. Petersburg, 1912-1916.

—— "Pis'ma is Sibiri" (Letters from Siberia), in *Novoe Slovo*, II, 7-49 (1907).

—— Sobranie sochinenii (Collected Works). Marks edition. St. Petersburg, 1900-1904.

—— Sobranie sochinenii (Collected Works). Gosisdat edition. Moscow and Leningrad, 1931.

Chekhov, Mikhail. Anton Chekhov i ego sujety (Anton Chekhov and His Themes). Moscow, 1923.

—— Vokrug Chekhova (With Chekhov). Moscow, 1933.

Chekhovskii sbornik. Chekhov i ego sreda (Chekhov Miscellany. Chekhov and his environment) edited by Bel'chikov. Leningrad, 1930.

Cheney, Sheldon. The Art Theater. New York, 1925.

—— The Theatre: Three Thousand Years of Drama. London, 1929.

Chentzov, N. M. Vosstanie dekabristov (The Revolt of the Decembrists). Moscow, 1929.

Coquelin, Constant. L'Art du comédien. Paris, 1894.

Craig, Edward Gordon. On the Art of the Theatre. Chicago, 1912.

—— The Theatre Advancing. London, 1921.

—— Towards a New Theatre. London, 1913.

Croce, Benedetto. Aesthetic as Science of Expression and General Linguistic. London, 1922.

Cuzzer, Otto. "Il pessimismo di Antonio Cecof," in *Cultura*, Anno III, pp. 115-19 (1923-1924).

Davydov, I. Amoralism Nietzsche i idea dolga (Nietzsche's

Bibliography

Amoralism and the Conception of Duty). St. Petersburg, 1905.

Derman, A. "Tvorcheskii portret Chekhova" (Sketch of Chekhov). Moscow, 1929.

Drisen, Baron Nikolay. Sorok let teatra (Forty Years of the Theatre). Petrograd, 1915.

Duclos, Henri Barnard. Antoine Tchekhov, le médecin et l'écrivain, thèse pour le doctorat en médecine. Paris, 1927.

Duesel, Friedrich. Maxim Gorki und Anton Tschechow. Berlin, 1922.

Duncan, Isadora. My Life. New York, 1927.

Dupuis, Ernest. Les Grands Maîtres de la littérature russe au XIXe siècle. Paris, 1897.

Feider, Val. A. P. Chekhov, literaturny byt (A. P. Chekhov, Compilation). Leningrad, 1928.

Figgis, John Neville. The Divine Right of Kings. Cambridge (England), 1914.

Flickinger, Roy C. The Greek Theatre and Its Drama. Chicago, 1922.

Gerhardi, William. Anton Chekhov. New York, 1923.

Gershenson, M. P. Y. Chaadaev. St. Petersburg, 1908.

Gilyarov-Platonov, Nikita. Otkuda nihilism (The Origin of Nihilism). Moscow, 1904.

Godet, Pierre. La Pensée de Schopenhauer. 1918.

Goethe, Johann Wolfgang. Faust. Munich, 1925.

Gogol, N. V. "Mertvia dushy" (Dead Souls), in Sochinenia (Works), Volume IV. Brockhaus-Efron edition. Petrograd, 1915.

Golovin, Constantine. Russkii roman i russkoe obshchestvo (The Russian Novel and Russian Society). St. Petersburg, 1897.

Gorky, Maxim. "Anton Tchekhov: Fragments of Recollections," in Chekhov, The Note-Books of Anton Tchekhov, translated by S. S. Koteliansky and Leonard Woolf. London, 1921.

—— Lev Tolstoy, A. P. Chekhov, V. G. Korolenko. Moscow, 1928.

—— Moi universitety (My Universities). Berlin, 1923.

—— and Alexander Kuprin and Ivan Bunin. Reminiscences

of Anton Chekhov, translated by S. S. Koteliansky and Leonard Woolf. New York, 1921.

Graham, Stephen. The Gentle Art of Tramping. London, 1931.

—— Tsar of Freedom: the Life and Reign of Alexander II. New Haven, 1935.

—— Undiscovered Russia. London and New York, 1914.

—— The Way of Martha and the Way of Mary. New York, 1915.

Grot, N. Nravstvenie idealy nashego vremeni: Nietzsche i Tolstoy (Ideals of Our Time: Nietzsche and Tolstoy). Moscow, 1914.

Grube, Max. Geschichte der Meininger. Stuttgart, Berlin, and Leipzig, 1926.

Grusenberg, S. O. Arthur Schopenhauer, lichnost', myshlenie i miroponimanie (Arthur Schopenhauer, as a Man, His Philosophy, and His World Outlook). St. Petersburg, 1912.

Halm, Hans. Anton Tschechows Kurzgeschichte. Weimar, 1933.

Hauptmann, Gerhart. Gesammelte Werke. Fischer edition. Berlin, 1912.

Herzen, Alexander. Sochinenia (Works). Gosisdat edition. Petrograd, 1920-1923.

Hogarth Essays, The. Garden City (New York), 1928.

Hughes, Glenn. The Story of the Theatre. New York, 1928.

Ibsen, Henrik. Eleven Plays, with an introduction by H. L. Mencken. Modern Library edition. New York.

Istoria Rossii v xix vieke (History of Russia in the Nineteenth Century), a compilation by various authors. 4 volumes. St. Petersburg, 1907.

Ivanov-Rasumnik, Rasumnik Vasilievich. Russkaya literatura ot 70s godov do nashikh dney (Russian Literature from the '70s to Our Days). Berlin, 1930.

Izmailov, Alexander. Chekhov. Moscow, 1916.

Jaloux, Edmond. Figures étrangères, first series. Paris, 1925.

Kogan, P. S. A. P. Chekhov. Moscow, 1929.

Korff, H. A. Die Dichtung von Sturm und Drang in Zusammenhange der Geistesgeschichte. Leipzig, 1928.

Korolenko, V. G. "Anton Pavlovich Chekhov," in Volume I of

Bibliography

Sobranie sochinenii (Collected Works). Marks edition. St. Petersburg, 1914.

Koteliansky, S. S., translator and editor. Anton Tchekhov, Literary and Theatrical Reminiscences. London, 1927.

Lenin, Vladimir. Materialism and Empiro-Criticism. New York, 1927.

Leontiev, Constantine. Sobranie sochinenii (Collected Works). Moscow and St. Petersburg, 1912-1913.

Lessing, Gotthold Ephraim. Hamburgische Dramaturgie, edited by Julius Petersen. Berlin, 1916.

Listowel, William Francis Hare, Earl of. A Critical History of Modern Aesthetics. London, 1933.

Lynd, Robert. "Tchehov: the Perfect Story-Teller," in Old and New Masters. New York, 1919.

Maeterlinck, Maurice. The Blue Bird, translated by Alexander Teixeira de Mattos. New York, 1914.

—— "The Modern Drama," translated by Alfred Sutro, in The Double Garden. New York, 1909.

—— Théâtre. Brussels, 1910-1912.

Malaya sovietskaya encyclopedia (The Little Soviet Encyclopedia). Moscow, 1929.

Markelov, G. "Filosofia Nietzsche kak kulturnaya problema" (Nietzsche's Philosophy as a Culture Problem) in Mir Bozhii, Oct., 1903, pp. 197-213; Nov., 1903, pp. 145-60.

Matthews, Brander. The Development of the Drama. New York, 1919.

Meyerhold, Vsevolod. O teatre (About the Theatre). St. Petersburg, 1913.

Mikhailovsky, N. Sochinenia (Works). St. Petersburg, 1914.

Mirsky, Prince D. S. "Chekhov and the English," in The Monthly Criterion, VI, 292-304 (1927).

—— Contemporary Russian Literature. New York, 1926.

—— A History of Russian Literature. New York, 1927.

Nietzsche, Friedrich. Also sprach Zarathustra. Leipzig, 1922.

—— Die Geburt der Tragödie aus dem Geist der Musik. Leipzig, 1872.

—— Jenseits von gut und böse. Leipzig, 1930.

Opalov, V. Chekhov v Krymu (Chekhov in Crimea). Simferopol, 1930.

Bibliography

Ovsianniko-Kulikovsky, Dimitrii N. "Istoria russkoy intelligentsii" (History of the Russian Intelligentsia), Volumes VII and VIII of Sobranie sochinenii (Collected Works). Moscow, 1923-1924.

Pares, Bernard. A History of Russia. New York, 1928.

Pascar, Henriette. Mon théâtre à Moscou. Paris, 1930.

Paulsen, Friedrich. "Arthur Schopenhauer kak chelovek, filosof i uchitel'" (Arthur Schopenhauer as a Man, a Philosopher, and a Teacher), in Mir Bozhii, Jan., 1902, pp. 101-23; March, 1902, pp. 106-39.

Plekhanov, Georgii. Essays in the History of Materialism, translated by Ralph Fox. London, 1934.

—— Introduction à l'histoire sociale de la Russie, translated into French by Mme Bartault-Plekhanov. Paris, 1926.

Pokrovsky. Kriticheskaya antologia (Critical Anthology). Moscow, 1907.

Potapenko, I. N. His recollections, in Niva, June, 1914, pp. 510-15; July, 1914, pp. 531-38, 551-57.

Russkii biograficheskii slovar' (Russian Biographical Dictionary). St. Petersburg and Moscow, 1896-1918.

Sayler, Oliver M. The Russian Theatre. New York, 1922.

Schopenhauer, Arthur. Métaphysique et esthétique, translated into French by Auguste Dietrich. Paris, 1909.

Selivanov, Vl. Dekabristy (The Decembrists). Leningrad, 1925.

Sergeyenko, Piotr. His recollections of Chekhov, in Niva, Oct., 1904, pp. 203-72.

—— Tolstoy i ego sovremenniki (Tolstoy and His Contemporaries). Moscow, 1911.

Shcheglov, Ivan. His recollections, in Niva, June, 1905, pp. 227-58; July, 1905, pp. 390-424.

Shchegolev, P. E. Alexeyevskii ravelin (Alexey's Ravelin). Moscow, 1929.

Shestov, Lev. Dostoyevsky i Nietzsche (Dostoyevsky and Nietzsche). St. Petersburg, 1909.

—— Nachalo i kontsy (Beginnings and Ends). St. Petersburg, 1908.

Sobolev, Yurii. Moskovskii Khudozhestvenny Teatr (The Moscow Art Theatre). Moscow, 1929.

—— Na zarie Moskovskago Khudozhestvennago Teatra (The Dawn of the Moscow Art Theatre). Moscow, 1929.

Bibliography

Soloviev, Vl. Krisis zapadnoy filosofii (The Crisis of Western Philosophy). St. Petersburg, 1874.

Stanislavsky, Constantine. Moya zhizn v iskusstve. Moscow, 1926. This book has been translated into English by J. J. Robbins as My Life in Art. Boston, 1924.

Strannik, Ivan. La Pensée russe contemporaine. Paris, 1903.

Suvorin, Alexey Sergeevich. Dnievnik (Diary). Moscow, 1923.

Teleshov, Nikolay. Moskovskii Khudozhestvenny Teatr (The Moscow Art Theatre). Moscow, 1929.

Tolstoy, Leo. Dnievnik (Diary). Moscow, 1916.

—— Sochinenia (Works). Moscow, 1903.

Tzertelev, Prince Dimitrii Nikolaevich. Aesthetika Schopenhauera (Schopenhauer's Aesthetic). St. Petersburg, 1900.

Volzhsky. "Dostoyevsky i Chekhov" (Dostoyevsky and Chekhov), in Russkaya Mysl', V, 33-42 (1913).

Vyshnevsky, A. L. "Kak nachinalsia Moskovskii Khudozhestvenny Teatr" (How the Moscow Art Theatre Began), in Novy Mir, pp. 200-211 (1928).

Wagner, Richard. Prose Works, translated by William Ashton Ellis, especially "The Art-Work of the Future" (Volume I) and "Opera and Drama" (Volume II). London, 1893-1899.

Williamson, C. "The Ethics of Three Russian Novelists," in The International Journal of Ethics, XXXV, 217-37 (1925).

Index

Index

Braha (composer), 111
Brieux, Eugène, 160
Brusov, Valerii, 196
Bunin, Ivan, 139, 176, 193
Burenin, Victor, 191, 192
Butler, Samuel, 110
Butova, N. S., 178
Byzantium (Byzantine Empire), 63, 65, 146, 147

Caesars, 63, 147
Capitol, 131
"Catastrophe, The," 144
Catherine the Great, Empress, 62
Caucasus, 87, 91
Cervantes, Miguel de, 26
Chaadaev, P. Y., 65, 66
Chaliapin, Fedor, 197
Chauve Souris, 197
Chekhonte, Antosha (pseudonym of Chekhov), 20, 21, 25, 27, 29, 31, 36, 42, 44, 48, 55, 140, 179, 184, 194, 206, 219, 220
Chekhov, Alexander Pavlovich, 18, 20, 23, 32, 35, 36, 39, 41, 42, 76, 78, 134
Chekhov, Anton Pavlovich, birth, 11; childhood, 11-22; education, 15-22, 25-27, 35, 42; visits to his grandfather, 22; horseback journey across steppe, 24-25; illness, 24-25, 37, 44-45, 54, 81-82, 92, 93, 125-27, 137-38, 166, 192-95, 198-99, 206, 215-19; removal from Taganrog to Moscow, 29-30; visit to Voskresensk, 42; medical practice, 42, 43-45, 55, 98, 105-6; vacation at Babkino, 45-48; visits to St. Petersburg, 49-50, 82, 97-98, 99; visit to Theodosia and journey through Caucasus, 87-88; estate in Luka, 92; journey to Saghalien and the Far East, 93-97, 98; journey with Suvorin to Italy, 99-102; purchase of Melikhovo, 103; life on the Riviera (also in France and in Italy), 128-32, 135, 181-83, 192; removal to Yalta, 137-38; visits to

Moscow, 180, 193-96, 198-99, 206-16, 217; marriage to Olga Knipper, 180-82, 193-95; birthday celebration (1904), 214-15; at Badenweiler, 215-19; death, 219; burial, 219-20. For works and for relations with others, see individual entries
Chekhov, Iegor Mikhailovich, 22
Chekhov, Ivan Pavlovich, 42, 99, 168, 183, 194
Chekhov, M. M., 24
Chekhov, Mikhail Pavlovich (Misha), 26, 35, 37, 49, 82, 93, 111, 113
Chekhov, Nikolay Pavlovich, 17, 21, 23, 36, 37, 88, 92, 115, 207
Chekhov, Pavel Iegorovich, 11, 12, 14, 15, 23, 31, 104
Chekhova, Evgenia Yakovlevna, 11, 17
Chekhova, Maria Pavlovna (Masha), 24, 97, 111, 138, 166, 178, 193, 218
Chekhov Theatre, *see* Art Theatre
Chernyshevsky, Nikolay, 68
Cherry Garden, The, 25, 29, 79, 92, 150, 153, 181, 190, 198, 200-15, 220
Chetyi Minei (Menologia), 13, 25
Chicago, 96
Childhood, 141
"Children, The," 142, 143
China, 95
Chirikov, Evgenii, 176
Chopin, Fréderic-François, 88
"Chorus Girl, The," 40
Chronegk, Ludwig, 159
"Cloak, The," 129
Comédie Françoise, 122
Constantine XII, Emperor of Byzantium, 146
Constantine, Grand Duke, 63
Constantinople, 146, 148
"Cook's Wedding, The," 141
Cosmopolis, 131
Cossacks of the Don, 22
Craig, Edward Gordon, 161

Index

Index

Index

Index

Index

Index

Index

Venice, 99, 100, 102
Veresaev, Doctor, 43, 136
Verlaine, Paul, 116, 196
Villa Fredericke (Badenweiler), 218
Village, 141
Villiers de l'Isle Adam, 196
Vologda (province and city), 65
Voltaire, 112, 173
Voskresensk (town), 42, 43, 183
Voskresensk, Gate of (Moscow), 30
Vutsinas, Nicholas, 15, 16, 92
Vyshnevsky, A. L., 167, 173, 176, 177

Wagner, Richard, 160, 174
"Wallachian Legend, The," 111, 112
War and Peace, 70
"Ward No. 6," 90, 106, 108, 112, 151
Warsaw, 63
Westernizers, 64-66

"Wife, The," 149
"Witch, The," 55
"Women Folk," 128
Wood Spirit, The, 117-18, 168, 175
Word of the Regiment of Igor, The, 104
World of Art, The (Mir Iskusstva), 127, 196

Yalta (Crimea), 137-39, 153, 168, 175, 176, 177, 180, 192, 193, 194, 195, 198, 199, 216, 217, 218
Yaroslavna, The Lament of, 104
Yasnaya Poliana (Tolstoy's estate), 109
Yenissey (river), 207
Yermolova (actress), 35

Zaïka (The Stutterer), 26
Zheliabov (leader of Narodnaya Volya), 61
Zhukovsky, Vasilii Andreevich, 67
Zola, Emile, 132-34, 160